SEVEN SEVEN
7X7 PEAKS 7X7 ISLANDS

CLIMBED AND WRITTEN BY NIGEL VARDY

Cover design and book design by Neil Coe
First published in 2011

Ecademy Press

48 St Vincent Drive, St Albans, Herts AL1 5SJ
info@ecademy-press.com
www.ecademy-press.com

Printed and bound by:
Lightning Source in the UK and USA
Printed on acid-free paper from managed forests. This book is
printed on demand, so no copies will be remaindered or pulped

ISBN 978-1-907722-27-1

CONTENTS

*"It's the work that counts,
not the applause that follows"*

ROBERT FALCON SCOTT

ACKNOWLEDGEMENTS

I would like to thank the following for their support, love and kicks up the bum...

My Mum and Dad for all their support and tea!
My big sister Amanda for rebuilding me on a regular basis.
Jamie and Clare Glazebrook for their undying friendship.
Ian and Jean Henderson for all the laughter, beer and pies!
Terra Nova Ltd for their support.
Rob Edmonds for squeezing ski boots onto what's left of my feet.
Martin Moran for his professional help in guiding me back into the mountains.
Alison Musgrove at Nottingham City Hospital for keeping my feet going.
Toby, Holly and Rupert Cross for their friendship, patience and love.
Paul Walker at Tangent Expeditions.
Craig Coates for putting up with me in an Arctic blizzard.
Jaime Vinals for giving me the Seven Islands challenge. (All this is your fault!)
Liz Roche for her patience, medical help and book buying.
Phil Poole for being a great tent mate when the chips were down.
Diane Leesmith for being a bloody great friend.
Dave Pritt at Adventure Peaks.
Sibusiso Vilane – My friend, you are the best!
Roanne Finch for allowing me to use her research on Everest.
Tina Moult for loving and supporting me through some of the darkest times.

Piers, Debbie and Helen Bostock for their friendship and sound advice.

Colletts Mountain Holidays.

Katrina Whitaker, Miles Hilton-Barber, Paul Booker and Kaye Booth for making sense of it all.

Mindy Gibbins-Klein and Ecademy Press for help in producing this book.

...and finally...

Kara, my 1977 VW Bay Window Camper. The best office a man can have...

PREFACE

When you accept a challenge to cross the world, risk life and limb, set records and face the consequences, you should not do it lightly. You should take a long, hard stare at it and consider what you are undertaking, but more importantly why you want to do it. By the time I had accepted my challenge it had already begun, but I was determined to see it to the end. It all came from one conversation in a tent, which was to rule my life for the following five years.

Jaime Vinals is an incredible climber from Guatemala. He was in the Arctic, or more specifically on Baffin Island, to climb its highest point and continue on a quest to climb the highest points on the world's seven largest islands. This immediately caught my mind as something I could do despite my frostbite injuries. Mt McKinley had robbed me of all my toes, fingertips and nose only four years before, and I struggled to walk long distances or climb extreme mountains. I had to pamper my wounds continuously to keep them in one piece and couldn't risk further damage. People told me that I should be relaxing on a beach and taking life easy, but that's just not me at all.

The peaks ranged from glaciated Arctic mountains to jungle clad tropical volcanoes. How these differing climates would hurt my already battered skin grafts and scars I didn't know, but I was willing to find out the hard way. My life needed a purpose, a goal, and this was it. My soul had been in the wilderness and it needed direction and order, two things I thrive on. I had no idea where the challenge was going to take me, but I didn't care. The end seemed a long way away and there were plenty of bridges to cross, physically, financially and emotionally.

Jaime was almost at the end of his journey, having only

Greenland to visit after Baffin Island, and then he was off home to his family. As his adventure was ending, mine was just beginning...

CHAPTER 1
THE PENNY ICE CAP
BAFFIN ISLAND
APRIL/MAY 2003

"It is a mistake to look too far ahead. Only one link in the chain of destiny can be handled at a time"

SIR WINSTON CHURCHILL

The rain was beating on my office window as I sat silently surfing the web. It was late at night and I was wondering what to do with my life. Post-expedition blues had set in since my recent return from Nepal and I was desperate to travel again. I sipped on a glass of whisky, closed my eyes and sat back in my chair. "What the hell is wrong with me?" I thought. "You've only just got home from one trip. Give yourself some time Nige." The room was in darkness, save for the white light of my computer screen and the flashing beams of car headlights as they shone through the blinds. There was a ping as a new e-mail came in. I lazily opened an eye and clicked on it. It was from my friend Craig in Yorkshire. "Nige, I'm thinking of going to Baffin Island next year and wondered if you might be interested?" I sat straight up, put down my glass and began to read intently. There was little information to hand, so without much thought I replied, "Yes mate, send me some more details!" I had always worked on what my instinct told me, but had no idea what I was about to undertake. I had been trying to get out to Baffin Island for years after reading of its mountains and history and watching a few TV programmes, but circumstance and severe injury had stopped me time and time again. It seemed my chance had finally come.

The plan was to ski tour towards the Penny Ice Cap and climb Tete Blanche, the tallest peak on the island. I searched for maps, but came up with little, although I did manage to read some reports from climbing magazines, but they were very sketchy. "Sod it, just go," I quietly said to myself and sent confirmation details to Craig. My family didn't like the prospect of me going off again, but my mind was sold.

Situated to the north-east of Hudson Bay, Baffin is one of the world's largest islands and is covered in a wilderness of ice – it is my kind of country. Over the winter of 2002/3 I trained hard and worked hard to both prepare and pay for the trip.

My mind and body were for adventure, but my heart was somewhere else. A few months before I left I had met a woman who truly loved me, and I her. It is rare in my experience to find anyone who will put up with my climbing adventures, but she was special. Debbie thought my expeditions fantastic, and with a bursting heart I packed my bags for the ice of Northern Canada. As ever with expeditions, the day of departure suddenly loomed and no matter what preparation I had done or training I had undertaken I never felt quite ready. The day before I left, my sister Amanda was helping me hang curtains in a newly decorated bedroom. Downstairs the house was chaotic as my entire family was here for my farewell. Many tears were shed as one by one they left. Upstairs, alone, sitting on my bed was Debbie. I felt awful leaving her and we cried in each other's arms for what seemed an age before she wished me farewell. "Don't worry, I'm coming back in one piece," I said. "You'd better do!" she replied. I smothered her with gifts and she gave me a card to open for every week I was to be away. Goodbyes are some of the most difficult things we do in our lives and are never easy. She didn't want to go, I didn't want her to leave, but it had to happen. With glazed eyes on both sides she crunched over the gravel to her car and drove away. I waved her goodbye from the front door and suddenly found myself alone; alone for an evening of reflection, peace and the odd whisky to calm my nerves. I was already homesick and broken hearted and I hadn't even left my own home. Love can do the strangest things to a man.

Craig was waiting for me at Heathrow, along with other members of our party. This was not a two-man adventure, but organised through Paul Walker of Tangent Expeditions. Some hardcore adventurers might think this a bit soft, but getting into the ice fields of Baffin would be hard enough as it was, never mind the climbing, skiing and loadhauling. I began to learn new names, something I am terrible at. Adrian, Paul, another Nigel (that's easy enough) and so on.

Long distance air travel is something I have got used to over the years, but I've never enjoyed it. Being 6 2 in economy class is hardly comfortable, but I find a few gins and sleep deprivation from the night before a good cure for boredom. We flew via Ottawa, into Iqaluit – the capital of Baffin Island – before a last leg to the small settlement of Pangnirtung. We had left the jet age far behind and the propellers on our last flight were deafening, but I looked out of the window and stared into pure silence. We were crossing ice fields and Arctic tundra at low level. There was not a sign of life for mile after mile and my mind emptied itself into the desolation. This was what I came to places like this for – to rid myself of the western world and its trappings. The ice was neutral, the air fresh and not a symbol of man in sight. We came alongside the Cumberland Sound and soon touched down in what looked like a prefab village against a frozen sea. That's exactly what Pangnirtung turned out to be – rows of 1970s wooden buildings built against a decaying Hudson Bay Company Whaling Station fronted by miles of sea ice. The town had been created to take the Inuit away from their nomadic lifestyles and put them into strict settlements. Why we, as a people, ever do this to ourselves I will never know. How many times in the name of "civilisation" have we moved people from lands they have inhabited in harmony with nature for centuries? I believe that tribes, peoples and nations should be able to live as they wish, provided they don't enforce their ideas and beliefs on others.

My warm European heart froze as I walked out of the plane and into the fresh Arctic air, but I felt happy to feel the cold tearing through my chest. Cold is my favourite climate, but it had cost me dear a few years before and one thing kept nagging at my mind: "You've already had frostbite Nige, how will you cope on an Arctic glacier? Are you stupid?" It was my 34th birthday and I had been through enough change in my life already. I was in no mood for more. This was the main reason my family had felt so strongly about me coming here, but I had to come. Something inside was urging me on.

Early the next morning six Ski Doos appeared. Their deafening roar shattered the silence, but one by one they switched off their engines and peace prevailed, at least for a while. The leader Charlie came over and said hello. He was broadly built, but softly spoken, and his smile and handshakes were welcomed by everyone. He turned and began to shout in Inuktitut (the native tongue) and waved vigorously to sort his team out. Each Ski Doo was towing a wooden sledge full of gear, which is where I expected my bag to go, not me. I expected to be on the pillion seat. How wrong I was. Our party of twelve was divided into six pairs, with Craig and myself put together. We had been warned to dress well and we soon found out why. We both resembled Michelin Man and were beginning to boil as we stood around, but at 40 mph over the ice, the cold soon began to cut through our clothing. Our Ski Doo driver was slight, tanned, happy and quite mad. He wore large headphones, which we later found out blew AC/DC loudly into his ears. Perhaps it was to blank out our screams?

The formation left Pangnirtung in a plume of ice and headed straight across the Sound at full speed. I find it hard to describe the incessant banging, crashing and landing of a high-speed sledge, but I'll do my best. Imagine a tall-sided coffin on runners, held together with thin rope, doing 40 mph over a sea of frozen waves and sastrugi. Then throw yourself and a good friend in there and hang on for grim death. Oh, I almost forgot, you need some kit to fly around you, a couple of caribou skins for comfort and the understanding that this thing could break up at any moment. After only a few minutes that's exactly what it did as a runner came away. Our Inuit driver was highly skilled and stopped in a flash, mended the sledge and we were on our way again. The sledges were built to be flexible and easy to repair – exactly what is needed in such a climate. Western culture can learn so much from the traditional peoples of the world when it comes to survival and environment. We turn up clad in Gore-Tex galore, showing off manufacturers name badges as medals of honour, when we haven't set a foot on the ice. The Inuit's had lived here for centuries in skin and fur and done very well for themselves.

Craig and I took it in turns to be in the back of the sledge. That seemed to be the better ride whilst the front did more of the banging. We swapped at breaks and anywhere we slowed down, fearing a comical somersault into the glacier if we got it wrong, but we survived. We had met years before through Operation Raleigh expeditions and were great friends. We shared many things in common – climbing, travelling and work (as we were both in electrical engineering) – but there was something else – we were both in love. Our respective girlfriends were thousands of miles away, but in both our hearts. It might sound a bit cheesy or soppy, but it affected us in our own personal ways.

You might think that a Ski Doo would go anywhere in a place like Baffin, but it has one major enemy – sheet ice. The rubber track is delighted to drive over snow, but skids all over the place on ice. Time and again we got out of the sledge, donned crampons and pushed. At least it warmed us up, before we jumped aboard again and set off. I was glad of the work as my fingers and toes were beginning to suffer. No matter what I wore, the cold always seemed to find a way in and physical exercise was the best cure I knew.

At our lunch stop I experienced one of those strange things that happen when you travel the world. It seems the favourite food of the Inuit that day was raw Arctic char (expected) and Wagon Wheels (not expected). Still, they are both easy to chew at −10 °C!

There was nothing around us for miles except ice and the occasional rock sticking through. A few birds passed high overhead, but no other sign of animal life could be seen. The beauty of places like this grabs me every time; the emptiness is sheer peace, the desolation brutal.

About forty miles and eight hours after our departure we arrived at what was to be base camp. We were alongside a frozen lake with huge ice faces looming over us on two sides. To the north lay the way out – the main glacier into the interior. To the south was the way home. The gear was piled up and one by one the Ski Doos left, their drivers waving as they disappeared into the distance. They would be back in eighteen days no matter what, and we had to be ready! Complete silence was beautiful after the day's battering, but there was work to be done with a camp to build and gear to repack. The sun was only tepid with its warmth, but plenty of hauling soon warmed my icy hands and feet. They had suffered all day and ached incessantly; not ideal for someone who has lost toes and fingers to frostbite. Tents appeared and slowly people retreated into them for the night as cold shadows crept across camp. I struggled with the stove due to the biting cold and Craig cooked our first meal. I felt a little hopeless and tried to balance the workload by sorting food and kit. I just couldn't sit there and watch.

Next morning brought the start of pulk pulling. Before you ask, a pulk is a sledge designed specially to be towed behind you on a body harness. Inside you place everything you need for the next three weeks, and I mean everything. There's no resupply here. You take it, you pull it. Similarly, you forget it – tough luck! The first day is always a bit of a faff as people pack, repack, jump, sit and leap onto the sledges to get it all in, but as time progresses we eat the weight down.

We broke camp and headed off up the glacier. A recent north wind had blown much of the snow off the ice, leaving a glass-like surface exposed to the sun. We made slow progress on our crampons. They squeaked and grated on the ice as I pulled my 150 lbs behind me, but at least we were on our way. In gentle procession we climbed the first slope and entered the main glacier system.

You may think ice slippy stuff, but thousands of tiny stones were strewn across its surface, and dragging the pulk soon made me sweat, swear and curse. It would run, then not, and then run again. People have described this phenomenon as like dragging a bath over a sand dune, and I soon realised what they meant. After a couple of hours my harness began to chafe my hips and shoulders, but with some adjustment it felt better. These were the first tests of the trip and I hoped things would improve as I learned.

It's easy to look down at the floor when you are walking or pulling. I had seen enough people doing it in my native Derbyshire as they sped from place to place, in some sort of mad hurry, but please, I beg of you, look at your surroundings. Here I was staring at the ice, keeping in step with everyone, when I looked up and was amazed. Towering walls of dark granite, cut down the centre by a huge glacier, surrounded us on left and right. Stripes of stones, large and small, were draped on the surface like ribbons as the ice slowly moved downhill. The sky was pure blue without a cloud to be seen and the sun was burning. The cold of the morning had been replaced with searing heat, trickling sweat down my spine and melting sun cream into my eyes. Sunstroke can be a problem here, so I wore my best brimmed hat to protect my head and the highest factor cream I could get. I had suffered sunstroke in Guyana a few years before and knew its awful effects. I had almost been evacuated from the Amazon, but luckily recovered enough to continue. Here evacuation was a different and almost impossible outcome.

It got so warm in my Telemark ski boots that I had to dry my socks in the sunshine at every opportunity or face them freezing overnight. Clothing is a huge subject in the Arctic climate. Wear too little and you get cold, exposure or even frostbite. Wear too much and you sweat into the fabric. This can then freeze onto your skin. Neither choice is desirable.

A thin layer of snow began to appear underfoot and we swapped our crampons for skis. This made things considerably quicker and easier. As we changed over I realised that hardly anyone talked all day, or had I been in a dream world? Due to the weights we were pulling our minds had been focused on rhythm and pace. We also had to move in single file, roped in pairs due to the danger of crevasses. This made conversation difficult to say the least. When we did chat, I got to know Jaime Vinals a little better. This stocky Guatemalan had climbed Everest, travelled the world and was now in Baffin. His English was good, my Spanish wasn't, but we worked things out ok. He was one of three Everest summiters on the trip and I felt quite overcome with my company. Jaime, however, was impressed by my stories and that I was still out there doing it.

We pulled hard for three days, daunted by the overwhelming height of the cliffs that dominated our path. They made navigation simple enough, providing an alley to follow towards Tete Blanche, but also funnelled the wind straight into our faces.

The expedition leader Paul seemed confident of a successful trip, but overnight the weather changed, delaying us a day on our approach. It cleared again, but a day later returned with a vengeance. Overnight a full Arctic blizzard began to blow. I awoke to hear the tent buffeting in the high wind and the guy ropes whistling. I peered outside to see nothing but white as the cloud and snow had dropped to ground level. Occasionally the red or yellow flash of a tent broke through, but was instantly smothered by the whiteness. There was nothing to do but batten down the hatches and await its end. Craig and I thought a few hours, perhaps a day at best, but we were to be very, very wrong.

The hours soon passed into a day, the day soon became another. The dense cloud and snow never left us and the stormy winds battered our tents incessantly. On the third day Craig inched open the tent zip and stuck his nose outside. "What's it like out there Craigy?" I asked. "Pants," he replied. That said it all. Thick snow was flying around, accelerated by the tempest, making outside life impossible for any period of time. You only left the confines of your tent for two reasons – to get supplies from your pulk and visit the toilet. Crouching down in −20 °C during a blizzard is a necessity which concentrates the mind. It's hardly what I'd call entertaining, but what choice do you have?

We piled snow against the windward side of our tents to protect them the best we could and changed tent pegs for skis and ice axes. We also had to keep digging the pulks out as they surrendered to deep powder drifts, before leaping back inside the relative shelter of the tent. Occasionally I heard a shout, as someone ventured outside into the maelstrom to tie down a guy rope or check on the others, but few dared; it just wasn't funny outside.

So what do you do for six days in a tent? Yes, we were stuck for almost a week under canvas as the world outside tore itself apart. Well, you eat, drink, sleep, eat, drink, sleep... At least we were stacked high in supplies and dug in well. Of this I was very glad. I had almost died a few years before in a mountain storm and bad memories were nagging at the back of my mind. Your own mortality becomes paramount when you have faced death, but to hear the wind whistling again and to feel the cold's icy grasp put mental shivers down my spine. I lay awake in the dark trying to face the fact that I was safe this time, but it cost me a few restless nights and much nervousness. Having an old friend beside me made all the difference though. Craig knew my injuries well and understood more than most what I was going through.

Forced inactivity was a problem. I tried to break the monotony by reading Michael Palin's "Pole to Pole" and plugging my ears into Chris Rea's "Dancing with Strangers", but they were only a temporary respite. The daylight was long and boredom set in very quickly. Playing cards became the major pastime, but when all you want to do is climb, being stuck inside your tent is very frustrating. I knew that going out and adventuring in such conditions was not only dangerous, but also probably suicidal. Frostbite has had me once already. If I became injured again the damage would be far worse as any recovered tissue from my first injuries would have surrendered its life easily. I had little more to lose and had no intention of facing my family with more stories, amputations and hospital appointments.

A tremendous camaraderie began to grow across the camp. Though few of us knew each other well, we had all been in the mountains before and knew what these conditions could do to both the body and the mind. Our six tents were only feet apart, but it might as well have been miles, so we began to look out for each other, swap books, even tents for a few hours to break the monotony of the same conversations. Paul ran a mean card table, which many of us joined. I was awful at cards, but didn't care. It was better than nothing and laughter rang out from inside his tent. It was here that I began talking to Jaime more and more. We seemed to click and were rabbiting on one day when he mentioned his reason for being on Baffin. "My friend, I'm here to climb Tete Blanche as the sixth peak in my seven islands challenge." I was intrigued. I had never heard of such a thing; sure I knew about the famous seven summits, but nothing else. Jaime had already climbed them and was moving on. His plan was to climb the tallest peaks on the world's seven largest islands. We talked more and more that day and I could feel myself getting drawn into the bizarre thought that I could do it too. "Has any British climber done this before Jaime?" I asked. He wasn't sure. "Then I must find out when I get home," I replied. "If not, I think I should give it a go." What was I talking myself into? Could I really fly across the world and climb from Greenland to New Guinea? Japan to Madagascar? It all seemed quite bizarre, but huge amounts of energy began to explode through my veins. There was one problem though. We still had to climb Tete Blanche!

Back in my tent I continued to think. My mind was racing away with ideas and I couldn't settle. Had I found another challenge after beating my frostbite? There was too much to consider here, but I would hold on to the idea Jaime had given me.

Craig and I talked incessantly about our love lives when alone in the tent. We had photographs and stories galore and were missing our girlfriends madly. I opened a card Debbie had given me and read it constantly. "Absence makes the heart grow stronger" it said and indeed our hearts were strong. I loved my adventures, but also wanted to be lying in Debbie's arms. The weather wasn't helping. When you are climbing you don't think about many things except getting to the top and back safely. When you are bored, sat in a storm, your mind begins to dwell on matters. Sometimes that's good, but it can also be very dangerous.

Four days in, a few people started to crack. Jaime was camped with John, a hard-climbing Kiwi, who had also summited Everest, but they were struggling to get on. Whether it was language difficulties or their personalities I wasn't sure, but something had to be done. The enemy was the weather, not the people. I donned my thickest clothing, clipped on my Telemark boots and wandered over to their tent. I knew John was a character who couldn't sit still, so I tapped on their tent and screamed, "John, fancy a ski for a couple of hours?" "Yes please, Nigel," came the reply. "Get your arse out here then and hurry up, it's bloody freezing," I replied. Visibility was good, but the wind was still hard. I grabbed my skis and after only a few minutes we were off, equipped for anything, just in case. It felt fantastic to be upright and burning a little energy. Being 6 2 in a two-man tent isn't easy when your friend is next to you and gear is strewn everywhere.

We decided to skin uphill for a mile or so and then ski home, which is exactly what we did. There was little room for conversation as the wind blasted our words away, but just to be outside was enough. The camp looked tiny in the distance, but we never lost sight of it and returned safely after a couple of hours. Jaime was very relieved!

Whilst we had been gone Craig got out of the tent and began digging a bunker into the snow, just in case. Shovels of powder were appearing skyward and being disintegrated by the wind, but we were both in the same mindset – we need to move, exercise and burn some energy and we loved it. The hardest thing was getting back into our tent, looking like snowmen, without covering our gear in powder! Having been in the fresh air for a bit, I suddenly noticed the stench rising from inside. Our enforced stay was turning us stiff and stale. Things would have to change!

Being the expedition leader, Paul had to make some decisions. The weather had shattered any chance we had of climbing Tete Blanche and we had to face facts. Well in life I'm a realist. Time was running out and we were still two days short of the mountain. So what were we to do? Conversations went here and there about this and that. People pointed at the areal photographs we were using as maps and gave their opinions. I hardly said a word, bowing to others' ideas. Eventually Paul suggested that should the weather stay poor, we should abandon Tete Blanche and try to climb the summit of the Penny Ice Cap if we had the time. It wasn't the greatest feeling I held in my heart that night, but what else could we do? Nature dictates the world in places like Baffin, not humans. We might think ourselves masters of the earth, but we are not.

The summit of the Penny Ice Cap (2200 m) is the highest point on Baffin, but hold on a minute, I thought Tete Blanche (2156 m) was the highest mountain? It is. For some unknown reason, the highest mountain and highest ice cap are separately recorded. This makes the Seven Islands challenge a bit odd. I would have thought that the highest point should be climbed, and why the Canadian mapping authorities had separated them staggered me.

The next morning opened with a symphony of ice blasting onto the tent, but by the interval a warming sun had entered the stage. People began to gather outside and looked aghast at one another. "Come on then, let's get going!" was the cry as we grabbed our kit, clipped into ropes and skis, and set off single file for the Penny Ice Cap. It looked a particularly uninspiring mountain over to our west, but it was better than nothing. It was 1:45pm and the usual cries of "How long to the top?" etc. rang out. I would just be happy to summit and warm up. My feet felt dangerously cold, but I was in no mood to run for my tent.

We were roped in two groups of six and cut a single pair of tracks through the snow. The speed was swift as everyone was desperate to stretch their legs and accomplish something from the trip. When you have laid out large sums of money, it's a little embarrassing to go home having done nothing.

Flat glacier soon turned into gentle slope and then steeper snow. We stuck on skins and began to sweat a little in our labour. The sun was burning and the wind only slight as the weather system that had dogged us so long left the stage and was gone. Around us the mountains rolled over huge glaciers and all was white, save the distant summits of Mts Thor and Asgard. These towers of granite stood out for miles – lonely sentinels in a sea of ice. I turned to my left suddenly and saw the peak we should have climbed – Tete Blanche. Its summit looked beautiful, pointed and unlike anything around it. It also looked a long way off. How I wished I could have been on her there and then, but it was not to be. I could not afford to harbour those kinds of emotions. The Penny Ice Cap was where I was and I had to focus on it.

The slope levelled off to reveal a huge plateau. It was the summit, although quite where you would plant your flag I'm not sure. There didn't seem an inch of difference over the acres of ice. After a couple of hundred yards we stopped and celebrated. Wherever the summit was, it was where we decided to stand. There were no screams of delight, no whoops or cries, but more a shaking of hands and a brew. The team may have been international, but the occasion very British. I opened my bag, drew out my large Union Flag and posed for a photograph.

I'm no nationalist, but I am very proud of my upbringing, my heritage and my country. The flag had travelled with me over many mountains, and I hoped it would for many more. Jaime joined me with his Guatemalan flag and some sponsors pennants for a few photos and we broadly smiled together as the cameras clicked. Sponsorship was something I had tried many times before, but failed miserably at. I had taken a simple decision early on to pay for my own adventures and not be governed by others. It was a hard choice as world climbing in an expensive business, but I took it. "I'm sorry we couldn't climb Tete Blanche, but this is higher, so it will do for me," said Jaime. His words were like music to my ears. If I was to take on the Seven Islands challenge this was one down, six to go.

The six-hour climb was topped with only a few minutes on the summit as the day was nearing its close. Though darkness hardly falls here in the summer, it was only early May and we had to scurry home. Our bodies were casting long shadows across the frozen waves of ice and the still air sat at −7 °C. My moustache had frozen solid and my nose felt icy. I couldn't risk losing it to the cold again. The tracks we made on our ascent were safe and easy to see, so one by one we set off at our own speed for camp. I'm no skier, but I try to Telemark as best as I can, loving the freedom that freeheeling gives. Craig's mountain skis soon launched him downhill at great speed, whilst I gently followed on, falling regularly. Soon the twelve of us were strung out over a mile or so, all in our own little worlds as the sunset illuminated the ice fields in an incredible crimson display. I think it was one of the most wonderful views I had ever seen in all my life. Rocky outcrops soaked in the light whilst the ice rebounded it in deep reds, purples and blues. The sky was a deep electric blue, almost rainbow-like in its saturation of colour and shade. It truly was inspiring.

After the downhill came the long flat slog to camp. I ran like a madman, my Telemark skis being to the advantage now, but I could not catch Craig. He was far too fit, determined and ahead of me. I slowed down and then stopped. There was no one around and I savoured a few private moments. Staring into the silence was like looking into my own soul, and it brought home a few truths. Why do we insist on living our lives at such a hectic rate, incurring stress and pain for little gain? We surround ourselves with mobile telephones, computers and push our physical limits with the hours we work. My life had altered after frostbite and though I had some of the modern trappings of the day, I made sure that I kept sufficiently distant from them all to at least look at what I was doing. Being in such a huge place as Baffin allowed me to empty my mind and leave all its pains on the ice to freeze out of my memory. Thoughts over – time to ski again. I worked hard and slid rather ungracefully into camp as darkness fell. I was covered from head to toe in frost, but I didn't care. I wasn't the first in or last, but kept a watch with a steaming cuppa in my hand as the stragglers came home. A crescent moon appeared as the final act before the curtain fell and the day was done.

The next morning, no one felt very enthusiastic for the hill, although a few of us attempted a local, unnamed, and as far as we knew, unclimbed peak close to camp. I skied in, changed Telemarks for crampons and climbed. The route was distinct enough, but loose rocks the size of cars told us to reconsider our adventure. One or two smaller ones tumbled downward and it was only a matter of time before we would dislodge something bigger. Thick cloud began to close in and we struggled to see a couple of hundred yards in the whiteout. With heavy hearts we retreated by crampon and rope to the glacier and skied home. Thankfully our tracks led us safely to camp. We were cold, tired and encrusted in ice, but at least we were safe and alive. Risks are easy to take out here, but impossible to justify. One simple slip could turn into an epic.

Painful though it was to admit, I knew the expedition was over and it was time to retreat to Pangnirtung and finally, home.

The three-day journey to our pick-up point was assaulted by thick snow showers and blustery winds, but the evenings were beautiful and we made our rendezvous in good time. It had been downhill all the way with light loads. Unfortunately my feet were suffering the effects of cold and the skin grafts were bleeding a little. It sounds dramatic, but it isn't. This was normal behaviour for toeless feet covered in patches made from my hips and groin. I had got used to their problems and dealt with them the best I could.

In typical fashion the weather broke on the final morning, bringing beautiful blue skies and warm sunshine for our Ski Doo journey home. Sure enough, Charlie and the boys appeared and took us on the bumpy ride across the ice to Pangnirtung with one Ski Doo held together by two tent poles and a piece of string. I felt little during the journey as being out on the ice had hardened me for anything, except the return to society. I have always struggled when I come home from expeditions. Life is much simpler in the wilderness, but now I had a purpose, to explore if the Seven Islands, Seven Mountains challenge was on. I didn't even know where to start.

In Pangnirtung we were treated to hot showers, good food and a strange glass-fronted thing in the corner of the room – the TV. I had forgotten its awful ability to destroy conversation, but then again, the first film on was Apocalypse Now!

One final thought before I cross the world again. I arrived home to find that Craig was a single man. Whatever had happened to his relationship I'm not sure, but I knew exactly where he was coming from. I was alone too. Debbie had left me because of my travelling ways. All the love I thought we had was gone. The fanfares I expected upon my return were silent. I sat alone and cried the summer away.

It might be fun this adventure lark, but it can do your heart no good at all...

CHAPTER 2
GUNNBJORNS FJELD
GREENLAND
MAY/JUNE 2004

*"I postpone death by living,
by suffering, by error, by mistaking,
by giving, by losing"*

ANAÏS NIN

After returning from Baffin Island I spent the next year researching the Seven Islands, Seven Mountains challenge. The British climbing community had never heard of it and so, unsurprisingly, showed little interest. One editor told me, "Well, it's just another challenge to climb some obscure mountains. No one will be really bothered." On one hand, I would agree, but on another I couldn't. I wasn't here to climb for what other people told me or said. I was here to climb for me. Once we start using our own time and pleasures for other people's benefit, well, we might just as well give up and go home.

Hard graft and working overtime gave me the funding to travel to Greenland. I chose Tangent Expeditions again after the excellent support they had provided on Baffin Island the year before. I trained through the preceding winter by climbing in Scotland and skiing in the Alps, before the spring melt thawed the snow away. I have never been one for gyms and fitness clubs, much preferring to be outside in the open air. One fear I had was my confidence. Five years had passed since my epic on Mt McKinley, yet I still struggled mentally to cope with my expeditions. Physically I was as good as I could be, but my mind wasn't the same. I had struggled to ski well on Baffin Island and knew that Greenland would be a much harder challenge. In the Alps I forced myself down slopes that I knew too much for me in the vain hope of improvement, but felt little better. I cursed and cringed, ached and stung, but fought with my feelings. I just couldn't let go. With a typical "Sod it", I had to feel good enough and get ready to face the trip.

At home, summer was just beginning, but I wanted to be on the snowfields of the Arctic again. I felt guilty leaving my parents though as my dad had just undergone a hernia operation and was struggling to get around. My mum took on the role of carer and housewife as I left for Stanstead via my sister's house in Peterborough.

The team assembled in the airport terminal and flew to Iceland, overnighted in Reykjavik and made final preparations in the small north-west settlement of Isafjordur. We were a small team of five – four clients and a guide – all experienced climbers or mountain skiers with many miles under our belts. Five was a good number as I find smaller groups of people easier to work with. I have always hated large crowds of people since I was a boy. They are noisy, distracting and without emotion or soul. Thankfully the German guys spoke excellent English, which helped no end as my language skills are reduced to only two – English and Derbyshire.

The small town of Isafjordur was situated in the bottom of a huge glacial valley on the north-west coast of Iceland. It had an airstrip, a ski slope, a small harbour and not much more. The towering fjord sides dominated everything around them and lit up beautifully in the evening light. Talking of which, there was to be little darkness for the next month, as summer was approaching and the skies were clear. On Greenland it would be even brighter as the snow reflected every sunbeam like a mirror. The air was still during that final night and not a ripple disturbed the harbour's tide. The fishing boats were silent and only an occasional gull flew by. It was idyllic, well to me anyway, but then again places usually are when you visit them. I wondered what it would be like to live there. Probably very different, particularly during the long, dark winter nights.

We were delayed overnight due to bad weather over Greenland and spent a quiet evening in the town, before getting the green light to fly early the next morning. We collected our gear and stood in a huge metal hangar facing the runway. Across the tarmac a twin prop landed and began to taxi towards us. Seconds later the noisy engines fell silent and refuelling began. We began to load our equipment before dressing ready for our glacier landing in the Watkins Mountains. The problem here was the temperature. Heat haze was rising from the tarmac and thick layers of fleece and down were hardly ideal clothing. I hid inside the shade of the hangar, embracing its cool air, and wandered around an impressive collection of vintage fire engines and 1960s American cars, which loitered in the corners. All seemed in excellent condition, hidden away from the ravages of the winter and its cold. I learned that many locals had bought them off US servicemen who had been based here since the 1940s. I suppose it's no different to folks at home having a little two-seater sports car in the garage.

The final customs clearance was given, the paperwork stamped and a gunslip was placed on the counter. It's not perhaps what many of you would be used to, but here it's the norm. Imagine yourself at the airport check in. "Have you packed your bags yourself sir?" "Yes." "Any firearms, sir?" "No." "Well, take this, it could come in handy." It might all seem a little scary, but in a world strewn with polar bears it's a useful bit of kit. Everyone but me backed off, but I was very happy to take the weapon. It was a WW1 US bolt action service rifle, chambered at .30 cal. Firearms have been part of my life since childhood and I had little fear and great regard for them. "Don't forget the ammunition," the customs man said and calmly handed me a box of twenty rounds. I signed nothing; he didn't take my name, passport number or details in any way and didn't look particularly bothered either. I threw the slip over my shoulder and walked outside towards the waiting plane.

The engines of the twin otter burst into life and we set off, northward, to cross the Denmark Straits to Greenland. The plane rumbled down the unmade runway, lifted off, took a left and was funnelled by the fjord towards the sea. I got my last glimpse of Iceland before the blue seas merged into the blue skies.

Conversations on small propeller driven aircraft are almost impossible, so I stared out of the window at the sea below. I'm notoriously travel sick and prefer to keep my thoughts to myself when I can. The waters seemed calm, endless and silent, away from the metal wing of internal combustion and noise. I find a strange kind of peace during these times, perhaps as a result of my mind trying to slow down my excitement at a new adventure.

After an hour of continuous blue I saw my first piece of floating pack ice. It looked rather lonely, but within minutes it was joined by hundreds, then thousands of small icebergs, which in turn merged into a sea of crazed white shapes, separated by thin stripes of clear, blue water. The summer melt was on and the pack was breaking up. Slowly it was sailing south, disintegrating as it went, save for a few of the larger slabs which might make the North Atlantic. I was so entranced by the pack that I almost missed the oncoming coastline and its huge peaks. They stood like a row of monstrous dragon's teeth made from ice cream dotted with chocolate chips. We flew between a huge pair of cliffs and cruised down valleys that had been carved out by millions of years of ice and weather. It's easy to feel daunted by such places, as your own self would be lost in a pin prick against the towers, but worse is to come when you are standing in the middle of a few hundred miles of ice. In the distance I saw just that – an established camp we were about to land against. It was a dot of black surrounded by a sea of brilliant white. In excellent English the Icelandic pilot requested us to fasten our seat belts before circling camp and giving us one of the smoothest glacier landings I had ever experienced. The twin otter slid gracefully over the snow, pulling a beautiful plume of white behind her skids as we began to circle the camp.

I wasn't sure what was going on, but the pilot was preparing a pair of solid tracks ready for takeoff. Sinking into the deep snow wasn't an option. Suddenly we stopped and the engines were cut. The door opened and the cold crisp air grasped at my lungs. I pulled on my sunglasses, jumped onto the glacier and sank up to my knees.

We unloaded our gear, stacking it in some resemblance of order in the snow. I sat on my kitbag and stared into the distance. Here I was, in the middle of the Watkins Mountains, sat on a huge glacier at almost 2200 m (the summit of the Penny Ice Cap on Baffin Island). Around me were huge ridges with peaks jutting skyward and four miles away was the prize – Gunnbjorns Fjeld. "Jaime you sod, will I ever forgive you for this?" I thought jokingly. That one meeting last year had set my soul on fire, but I had to remember that it wasn't a race. I hadn't the time or the funding for that, and anyway, the faster you run the, the quicker it ends.

Standing at 3683 m (12,083 ft) high, Gunnbjorns Fjeld is the highest peak in the Arctic and dominates the entire range. Called by the Vikings "Hvitserk" or white shirt, she was used as a navigation aid as the longboats followed the Greenland coast and made for North America.

The pilot drew a huge wooden hammer from the cargo hold and proceeded to tap every skid loose of the snow before firing up his engines and waving goodbye. Within moments the deafening blast was reduced to a dull drone and then nothing. We were alone and on our own for the next three weeks.

We built camp and packed the pulks for a supply run towards Gunnbjorns Fjeld. I shared a pulk with Phil (our guide), so it was super heavy, but I was buzzing and itching to go. The mid afternoon sun was blazing down, but all I wanted to do was power on towards my goal. I heaved and sweated, sang to myself to keep pace and pulled my heart out.

Mountains have a strange ability to look close, but be miles away. The summit seemed an afternoon's walk, but after four hours of hard slog we ditched our supplies, turned around and made for the tiny black dot down on the glacier. It was 8pm and still beautifully bright. I lay on the freezing snow and stared into the sky. What a place this was, huge, empty and beautiful. "What could possibly stop us or go wrong?" I thought. I was about to eat my words and feelings, as the ski home was ready to start. There was little in the way of crevasses, so we were allowed to get going in our own time and meet back at camp. Liz and Wolfgang set off at great speed and were soon almost out of sight. Ulli and I kept a steady pace as Phil kept a watchful eye over us. I began shakily and went downhill from there, in both ways. I fell again and again on the slushy, spring-like snow and made quite a fool of myself. Phil looked back probably wondering who this idiot was who obviously couldn't ski, and what the hell he was doing in Greenland. My alpine nightmare had come to fruition. What should have been a swift journey soon turned into a two-hour epic. I walked into camp embarrassed and with my head held low. No one seemed too bothered, but I spent the evening quietly beating myself up about it.

The next morning we struck camp and headed back towards yesterday's depot drop. I had slept badly in the blazing light and my eyes felt heavy. I had tried my head in my sleeping bag, but it was too hot, so I put my sunglasses on, but they kept me awake. I put a bandanna over my face, but it felt wrong. There was nothing I could do but get used to it. With gear in tow we headed out, Phil and I sharing the one pulk again. It felt like a lead weight as I tried to find some momentum, but it wasn't playing today. I had left the gun behind as the risk of polar bears here was nil, but still the weight was huge. Perhaps it was the snow, but little had changed in the world since yesterday – or had it? My irritation began to grow and bit-by-bit I wound myself up for no good reason at all. I had to concentrate on the job in hand and get a grip of the weight behind me, or risk losing it mentally. I began to sing silently to myself, which gave me timing and pace relevant to the work I was doing and distracted me from the pain in my shoulders. It seemed to work better with Queen than anything else I could think of and knew the words to, but a mountaineer singing "I want to break free" might be thought quite mad. Therein lies another part of my life. At least I didn't do Freddie Mercury impressions...

Phil took over half way and asked me to lead off and break trail. It sounds hard, but when on skis, the work is much easier. There were patches of deep snow, but I continued to sing to myself and followed the tracks made yesterday to our depot. Behind me the guys were strung out over a few hundred yards, but pulling well and looking strong.

At our depot I was given one of the most dangerous alpine weapons I knew – a snow shovel. As a young engineering apprentice I had spent months working with road gangs, digging up tarmac and concrete in the streets of my native Derbyshire. With a mischievous look in my eye I created a protective bunker for the tents the size of a gun emplacement. I had dug madly, loved every minute and was shattered. The altitude was kicking in and my breath was short. White clouds spewed from my mouth condensing icicles onto my moustache.

Soon the tents were up and the brews on. There was something about the roaring of a petrol stove which makes the world seem right when you are climbing. Perhaps it's similar to the feeling that an open fire gives on a starlit night in the wilderness.

I spent the evening rehydrating from the day's exploits, but finished with a dram of whisky. I was bought membership of the Scotch Malt Whisky Society when in hospital years ago and had kept it up religiously. My kitbag contained a fine bottle of malt with which to share, savour the day and make Liz screw up her face and go "uurrgghh!"

I was greeted next morning by a tent burning with heat as the sun's rays turned up the wick. I flung the doors open to see another beautiful day and lit the stove. We had two choices, either make a trail and summit tomorrow, or go for it today. I knew my preference. I was out early, kitted up and ready to go.

Liz and I broke trail to the start of the summit ridge. I had to work hard to keep up with her, as she was incredibly fit and a competent alpinist. She had skied and climbed in America for years, but she had to temper her adventures with her life as a doctor in the UK. The rest of the gang joined us quickly enough and we split onto two ropes. Phil, Wolfgang and Liz on one, me leading Ulli on the other. I led off, kicking deep steps into the soft crystallised snow and scraping on the rock-hard blue ice, before walking out onto the magnificent summit ridge. For 360° around there was perfect visibility. Mountains jutted out of the enormous ice cap for miles and miles and miles. They seemed to go on forever. Between them was a sea of ice, only broken by occasional islands of rock. The sun was perfect and illuminated the stage for our final ascent to the summit.

The ridge was wide and plastered in solid snow. I led off for the last few hundred yards, but stopped short of the actual summit so that everyone could catch up. We took the last few steps together and exchanged smiles. Again, no whoops of joy or screams of laughter, just a few handshakes, photographs and of course my flag. Here she was with me again, on the Arctic's highest peak. Two down, five to go.

We only spent a short time on the summit before heading back for camp. I wasn't looking forward to it at all. Climbing and walking down in crampons was simple enough, but I faced the skis again with dread. Liz stayed with me and cracked jokes to keep me going until we could see camp in the distance. At that point she wished me goodbye and like a rocket sled, tore down the hill. I fell, skied, fell, skied, you get the idea, until I entered camp at 8:30pm. I was shattered, snow covered and embarrassed, but happy. In its own sort of way the rest of the trip was now a holiday.

Three days in and my mission was complete, but there was no chance of me sitting still. I was surrounded by beautiful mountains with supplies stacked around me and aching for climbing.

The weather broke and light snow began to fall from the overburdened white clouds. That didn't put me off climbing two virgin peaks over the next few days. Climbing where no one has ever been before is unknown at home, but in Greenland you are spoilt for choice. The peaks were tall, one demanding the ascent of a very exposed snow ridge, but the weather held and importantly the winds were light. The final moments felt incredible as I made the first ever footsteps in the snow, perhaps a feeling I may never experience again. The trip was going great guns, but as ever with many expeditions, there is always the chance that great danger is only around the corner...

A further part of the trip was to climb the second and third highest peaks in the Arctic, unimaginatively named Dome and Cone. We returned to base camp, re-supplied and undertook a two-day pull high into the next valley. All seemed well. Everyone was getting on, the weather was good and confidence was high. We set off for Dome, climbing it in a ten-mile-long skiing and crampon bashing day. The summit was as dramatic as Gunnbjorns Fjeld, but the climbing more sustained. We had to negotiate avalanche debris and serac fields on the ascent, but at least had tracks to follow home. Again I struggled with the return to camp and came in last. I didn't care. The stoves were roaring and the whisky ready. It was later on that things took a turn for the worse...

I hadn't been sleeping well and awoke in the night, but not because of insomnia. A shooting pain was stabbing across my stomach. I tried not to wince in case I woke Phil, but again and again the knife seemed to stab deeper and harder. I started to sweat, then freeze, then sweat again. Eventually I had to sit up, well I tried to, but the pain got worse if I attempted to move. The trouble was that I couldn't lie down any more as I now felt like puking up. I had forced myself into a half sitting position when Phil stirred and peered into the half light. "Are you alright mate?" he asked, but I couldn't reply as I had just been sick into my mouth and swallowed it back down. As my throat cleared I murmured, "No, is there a bag about? I'm going to throw up." There was a sudden rustling as Phil emptied some food sachets onto the tent floor and handed over the clear plastic bag. I didn't need any help in emptying the entire contents of my stomach straight into it. Both Phil and I were in a rotten position. We hardly knew each other, yet were trapped in a tent, high on a Greenland glacier as I threw my guts out. Phil was fantastic, kind and helpful as we sat by torchlight wondering what the hell was going on. He called Liz (always good to have a doctor on the trip), who took one look at me, laid me down and gently laid her hands on my stomach. Phrases like "Could be a virus" or "Have you eaten anything odd?" came from her lips, but they meant little to me. "Hold on," she said, "I'll get some tablets." She ran to her own tent and was back in moments with a vast selection of pills. "These should help." I swallowed them down, but within minutes they were sitting in the base of the filling plastic bag. Then came the sentence of the trip. "Do you still have your appendix?" she asked. "Yes," I croaked. "You're quite old for an appendicitis, but you never know..." I was 35 years old and had no idea most people who have trouble are free of the little beast in their late teens. Can you imagine how my mindset changed with that one sentence? I had gone from feeling ill to possibly requiring surgery! Liz tried her best to allay any fears I had, but there was no way I was going to take it, well, lying down. I tried to lie still for the rest of the night and sleep where I could, but morning soon came and Phil's words summed me up. "You look rough mate." Believe me, I felt it.

I couldn't go out with everyone else during the day and lay in my bag feeling particularly sorry for myself. Liz had managed to get some drugs into me and I did feel slightly better, but still not good. Phil left me a two-way radio with instructions to call if I needed help as they practised crevasse rescue further up the glacier. I felt alone and abandoned, but also a hindrance to everyone. When they returned I managed a smile, but was still rough. Dehydration was being a constant problem, but I staved it off with plenty of hot drinks. I did manage to eat something, but it was piteously little. The important thing was that it stayed down for at least a few hours, before I sat up in the night again and threw it back out.

The next day everyone went to climb Cone, leaving me alone in the tent again. I was improving, but not enough to join them. Mid afternoon a message came from the summit and by tea time, long snake-like curves were being cut through the snow as they gracefully skied home.

The next morning it was time to retreat back to base camp and consider my options. Liz seemed upbeat and wondered if I could still ski, but I ended up lying on her pulk as she skilfully descended towards camp. I did manage the flat walk home, but fell into my tent exhausted. The dilemma now was, did we go for a rescue or not? "Am I damned or is this just bad luck?" I wondered. Another air evacuation was hardly what I wanted, but I deferred any decision into Liz's hands. We sat in my tent and talked it over. The conversation was calm, honest and open. I felt a little better and had eaten some food. Liz said that I looked a little better, so we took the decision to stay.

The next morning Phil, Liz and Ulli began to make preparations for one final push to climb a little known peak called Outpost. I was offered a chance, but wondered about my condition. Saying that, by going I would be closer to the doctor and that sounded good. I was feeling better by the day, but still fragile. Still, adventure runs deep through my veins and I wasn't about to give up now. It was a risk I thought worth taking, but it wore me to the bone. We descended from base camp and climbed the beautifully named Silk Road Glacier before establishing our high camp. The weather was perfect and ice crystals glittered in the evening light as they fell silently onto the glacier.

Though we succeeded in being only the second recorded team to summit Outpost (2848 m), I was in such a state on the journey home that I had an out-of-body experience during the last mile to base camp. It was at the end of a long, steep drag and the weight of the pulk had taken its toll. My body may have been towing the sledge, but my soul was floating ten feet above the ground. I felt dreamy, pain free and thought that time slowed down, almost to a halt. It was a strange sensation that I will never forget and hope I will never repeat. The ten-mile pull home felt more like fifty and I barely had the energy to build the tent before I physically collapsed into it, half unconscious.

The next day we were flown back to Iceland on the first leg of our journey home. I felt quite well and joined everyone for an evening meal, but fell to pieces later the next day. I had to be ambulanced to Reykjavik hospital for tests and Liz joined me, giving the crew a full breakdown of my recent illness. I can never thank her enough for what she did. I must have looked a sight – three weeks without a shave, sunburned, emaciated and writhing with pain. I was scanned, X-rayed and prodded, but got no answers. What I hoped would be a quick visit suddenly turned out to be an overnight stay on IV antibiotics and fluids. I was then told that I must stay longer for more tests and monitoring. Everyone else had to depart for their respective homes and leave me safe in the doctors' hands. Phil and Liz brought me a few gifts and then said their goodbyes. My kitbags were deposited next door and I was alone. My heart fell as they left, but it raced madly as I tried to explain to my family what was going on. I fielded the usual questions about what was wrong with me and when was I coming home with "I don't know". It's not what I wanted to say, but I had little choice.

Lying alone in bed, in a foreign country is not the way I wanted the trip to end, but sometimes in life we have little choice. This was the second time I had suffered away from my family and friends, but it felt a little easier. The staff were excellent, the food good and the treatment second to none, but I felt abandoned and alone. All I wanted to do was go home to my own bed and suffer there.

I underwent test after test over the next three days before being discharged and taking the longest two-hour flight I have ever faced. The Icelandic medical staff were convinced that my appendix had burst, but were controlling it with drugs and told me to "see your own doctor when you get home".

My GP came to the quick conclusion that my appendix was

bad, but thought it now rumbling. "If you'd been here when it happened, we'd have taken it straight out, but now we'll wait and see," she said. That basically meant, "We'll wait until it tells us it's ready!" I was furious. Being a travelling man, I didn't want anything inside me that could blow up at any moment and cause real problems. I complained and got nowhere, but I had more mountains to climb before there was any chance of surgery...

CHAPTER 3
MT FUJI
HONSHU
SEPTEMBER 2004

*"He who climbs Mount Fuji is a wise man,
he who climbs twice is a fool"*

JAPANESE PROVERB

The day before I flew to Tokyo, I had an appointment at the local hospital about my appendix. I sat in a stark white consulting room on an uncomfortable plastic chair and looked blankly across the desk. There sat the consultant in a white coat and glasses, perusing my notes. This appendix thing had been going on for too long as far as I was concerned and a great deal of foot stamping had been needed to get me this far. Shooting pains still stabbed at me and a strange gurgling sound had begun to rise from my insides on a regular basis. There was lots of umming and ahhing, prodding and poking, followed by the occasional nod, but I was here for my health, not to see a plumber! Still with no answers, I left for Japan the next day, health problems or not.

I arrived in Tokyo and walked (yes walked) around the city for the day before heading west to climb Mt Fuji. This huge city bustles 24 hours a day, but has beautiful oases of peace and quiet in the temples and pagodas, which have now been surrounded by high rise concrete and steel. Simple paper lanterns adorn the verandas whilst incense drifts through the wind. For a brief moment you may be able to feel what the city of Edo once felt like, before you walk through the gates and back into the chaos of today. The heat was searing, the pollution chocking, but the journey was worth every minute.

I travelled the 100 km west to Fuji on a coach from the Shinjuku Bus Station in Tokyo. I was a giant among the many travellers, but still ended up squeezed onto a tiny jump seat in the central aisle. I must have looked a sight, but didn't really mind, as long as I got to my destination in one piece. My back hated the journey as the jump seat had little in the way of support. The coach rattled and shook, sending shock waves from the flimsy seat straight up my spine as we climbed over the hills and out of Tokyo. I spoke to no one, tried to doze and

On the summit of the Penny Ice Cap

Ski Ascent of Gunnbjornsfjeld

Prayers in a ruined temple on Mt. Fuji

Lows Peak - Summit of Mt. Kinabalu

hoped that I didn't miss my stop.

Eventually we pulled in at Kawaguchi-ko station. I creaked from all angles as I stood, hobbled forwards and almost fell down the steps into the street below. I scrambled for my bag and was left standing under a corrugated tin roof by a few shops as the coach left. The sunlight was fading as I scanned the electrically lit crowds for someone I knew. Fireworks, music and costumes galore were in full swing as one of the thousands of festivals held every year here was well under way, and I struggled to concentrate my eyes. Tall I might be, but I was bustled around as the crowds moved around the street. Eventually our eyes met. I had found my old friend Diane. We fought through the crowds wearing beaming smiles and embraced. We hadn't seen each other for a couple years, but she hadn't changed. Her smile was lovely and she still only came up to my chest! The world went silent for a few brief moments before the hustle and bustle of the world returned. Our huge bags were being bashed by the crowds so we forced our way to the main road, hailed a taxi and were driven round Kawaguchi-ko Lake to our hotel.

All evening we never stopped talking – there was a great deal to catch up with, what with her teaching and my travels. She had been living and teaching in Maizuru near Kyoto, whilst I had been set on my quest for the Seven Islands challenge, yet it was as if we had never been apart. We had met ten years before on an Operation Raleigh expedition to Chile and remained great friends. Friendship is something that can and does span continents and years. It is something as precious to me as life itself.

We were the only western faces in the hotel and tried to blend in as well as we could, but it wasn't easy. Though I had read up on Japanese customs, Diane had to help me with the more local niceties when it came to the finer side of greetings and table manners. Please don't get the impression that I was a thug from England, I'm quite the opposite and had no intention of offending anyone. If you ever visit Japan, you will understand…

I discovered here one of the technological delights of our modern age – the electric toilet. I was just used to sit, do, stand, wipe, flush. Not any more! As I sat doing my bit for Queen and country, I noticed a selection of knobs and switches attached to the side. Everything was written in kanji, so I hadn't a clue what I was doing and just set to work fiddling with them to see what happened. Firstly nothing, until I realised that the seat was getting warm. "Ok, so what's next?" I thought. More twiddling, when then suddenly a jet of water struck me right up the bum. I jumped up, gave out an "Oohh!" and sat back down again. Unperturbed, I persisted with my experiment to be finally blasted with warm air. I have never left a toilet so shocked and intrigued in my life!

Most people's image of Mt Fuji is a beautiful postcard shot of a perfect volcanic cone, capped in snow under deep blue skies. I was told that only happens a very few days a year. We were confronted with heavy cloud and very little in the way of a view. Apparently that was normal. We took an early morning bus out of Kawaguchi-ko and round the lake where I noticed hundreds of small boats bobbing in the water with fishermen sitting up on what looked like bar stools. "Seems a strange way to fish," I thought. "Still, they must know what they're doing." They seemed stable in the water and the fish seemed to be biting.

The bus drove past Kawaguchi-ko station and onto Fujiyoshida, the start of the Yoshida Route. We got off in what looked like a suburban street and began our ascent.

Within minutes we were in thick woodland on a straight gravelled path. It was hardly difficult stuff and I loved the way that the tourist guides portrayed the climb (if that's what you can call it) as difficult and dangerous. "Well, we'll see," I thought, but I held little optimism. The Yoshida Trail is the longest route up Mt Fuji, ascending from around 850 m to the 3776 m (12,388 ft) summit in around 11 hours. The altitude ensured an overnight stay, but I was in no rush. All was good with the world as far as I was concerned.

We entered the Fuji Sengen Shrine after a short walk. The air was filled with the sound of chanting and the smell of incense. It was the weekend and many people were out enjoying the sunshine. A family party were holding a christening and were decked out in their traditional kimonos, posing for photographs as we walked by.

The gravel soon turned to tarmac and we made great progress despite the burning heat. I was glad of any shade cast by the trees and hid in it whenever we rested. The path soon gave way to long, winding sets of steps. Hundreds long, they were hard on my long western legs, as I could never get the stride length I wanted. Diane did a little better, but we both found the never-ending flights a little tiresome. There was then a wonderful change as small, sometimes abandoned shrines came into view. I was surprised at their condition, knowing how particular the Japanese are about order and cleanliness. Standing stones carved with kanji characters stood in the undergrowth, slowly being consumed by trees and bushes. Many had a small path trodden down and the remains of a few incense sticks burned at their bases. They were not quite forgotten.

We walked through numerous torii gates and onto more steps as we ascended. The shrines got more and more beautiful and yet were still abandoned. Tall buildings covered in intricate wood carvings stood invaded by nature, yet still a small presence was there as candles, incense and sake had been left as an offering. I stood inside one and stared at the holes in the roof. The sun peered through them, casting smoky shadows across the cool air. Paper prayers waved gently in the breeze and water dripped from a beam. It all seemed so sad to leave this ornately constructed building to nature's whim. I left with peace in my heart to rejoin the trail and get the first view of Mt Fuji proper. She didn't look much more than a huge hillside, but peaks often do when you are too close. To truly appreciate a mountain you need to be miles away on a clear day, preferably on a sun terrace with a G & T! The trees were beginning to thin and the upper slopes of pumice and rock were showing their true colours. It was going to be a dusty and slippery end to the day.

Time had passed quickly and neither of us had noticed. By the time we reached the fifth station it was late afternoon and we were running out of time. I don't think either of us were dawdling, but facts are facts. Soon we would be walking in the dark. That didn't bother us though. Diane and I had spent three months together in Chile and gone through much worse that this. We had dragged heavy kit through rainstorms, lived on army rations and gone days without decent rest or recovery time. A few hours on a trail with a head torch hardly frightened us. Please don't think I'm sounding or meaning to be overconfident or full of myself here. Risk and its understanding have been a major part of my life. We were both fit, well organised in good weather on a well-marked path, walking towards an illuminated building. It's hardly rocket science to understand the dangers...

By 7:30pm it was pitch black. Our head torches cut the dark easily, but the path was bordered by sharp thorn bushes, which grabbed and scratched. The ground had turned from tarmac and stone to slidey pumice, which tore at my wounded heels. I'd had worse, but it still stung. Diane and I wandered almost silently upward, staring at the light of the huts above, which towered in a line towards the summit.

We stopped at the seventh station (2700 m) and dropped our bags outside, before sitting on a bench to look down the route. We were tired and breathing hard in the thinning air, but far from broken. We were covered in dust and sat down without a word, but understood each other perfectly. A simple meal and well-needed sleep was what we both needed. The hut was built in an alpine style with huge bunks and simple blankets. It was almost empty, silent and relaxing after the day's exertions and we took little rocking to sleep.

My watch alarm sounded at around 2am with its reliable and tinny sounding "beep, beep, beep". The hut was cloaked in darkness and deathly silent. Diane and I rose quickly and with few words dressed, ate and left. Early morning starts are part of mountaineering and I quite enjoy them, but to some folk they are the worst things out. Diane knew me well enough, as I knew her, and with little complaint we set off silently up the blackened slopes towards the summit. Within an hour I noticed her get slower and slower and thought the altitude was getting to her, but I was wrong. Her feet were struggling and the pain was becoming unbearable. Slipping and sliding on the pumice last night hadn't helped and her heels were done. Blisters were stinging and her skin was red raw. We sat down and faced a difficult situation. We were both leaders, used to giving orders and not receiving them. I wasn't happy leaving her; she was insistent that I should go on. There was no use in arguing. We were on a well-marked mountain path with plenty of huts and we were both experienced and adult. She decided to walk back to the seventh station and wait for me there. I wasn't happy, but agreed. She would be safe and I would be back soon. It was only a couple or so hours to the top and much less down. We hugged and slowly parted. I watched her descend for a few minutes before I turned and set off upward for the lightening sky.

There were few of us up there; in fact I could only see four other lights above me and none below. To the east the dawn was beginning to break and a layer of cloud began to settle underneath me. Slowly the sun rose and lit the sky red. It burned my eyes and cast my long shadow over the pumice slopes. I was still short of the summit, where I had hoped to see the dawn, but I didn't really care. The sky turned to yellow, then blue, as a perfect day seemed to unfold.

I passed the eighth station with its monstrous rampart-like defences and walls, before climbing the final steps towards the summit. Actually I must note that huge diggers were at the eighth station, carrying out some gigantic earthworks. The place looked more like a building site than a mountain hut. Concrete walls twenty feet high were cast to hold up the shaky footings of buildings, or stop the pumice from avalanching. It looked awful. Anyway, back to the mountain...

As I walked through the last torii gate the cloud began to fall and bring with it steady rain. "Typical," I thought. "You come this far and it chucks it down on you!" Still, there was little I could do. Rain is rain, wherever you go. As I walked the final few steps to the summit I had to search around for a cairn, because I couldn't see a thing. Visibility was a few feet, the wind steady, the cloud thick and the rain pouring. Mt Fuji, or Fuji-san as she should be known, last erupted in 1707 and today I was in no danger as it was too wet for eruptions! I set my camera on self timer and pulled out my Union Flag again. I took a few quick photos, folded my flag and sat down. I had some ghosts to put to rest.

I grew up in a small Derbyshire town in the 1970s and '80s. My grandfather was a shining light of decency, morality and hard work. He also despised the Japanese. During the

Second World War, he had fought in the Burma campaign and learned to hate his enemy with a vengeance. Was it the jungle conditions? Stories of the brutal treatment of prisoners of war? I'll never know. What I do know was that until the day he died, he would have nothing to do with the Japanese, have no appliance made there or even put up with them in the news or on TV. That hatred had been inbred into me from a young age, but I had grown up, understood our modern age and though I may have not forgiven them, I had let bygones be bygones. I wonder what he would have thought of me up there on the summit of Mt Fuji? He had died many years ago from the effects of years down the pit and from the malaria he had brought back from Asia in the 1940s. I opened my rucksack and from inside I brought out a Red Poppy I had saved from Remembrance Sunday the year before. I laid it below the summit, stood silently to attention and began the journey downward to Diane.

On my way down I came across one of the most incredible situations that I had ever encountered in the mountains. A middle-aged Japanese man was alone and struggling, I assumed with the altitude. I approached him to find an aerosol can stuck in his mouth. Instantly I was filled with curiosity. He pushed the can top and a sharp blast of oxygen filled his lungs at breakneck speed. Suddenly he got up and began to walk quite briskly, but like a clockwork toy, he got slower and slower until he sat down again. I know no Japanese, but I usually find a smile will break most language barriers. The chap seemed ok, but distressed about the amount left in the can. I was distressed that he was even here, relying on spray oxygen to deal with the altitude. "A wise man climbs Fuji once, a fool climbs it twice", so the proverb goes. More like "fools climb up where angels fear to tread".

I was soon on the decent route to the seventh station and there met Diane. She had managed a little more sleep and greeted me with a hug and a warm smile. Decisions on the hill are always difficult, but she had taken the right one and after a brief cup of tea we headed home with clear consciences. The route down was simple and the fifth station has a bus station. Actually it's a rather strange place the fifth station. A small village built in a Swiss style, halfway up a Japanese mountain. It's all a bit surreal. You can buy anything from a bento meal to an Alpine cowbell. We took the bus down and I took a final look back at the now clear peak. She hadn't been the greatest challenge of my life, but had provided an excellent opportunity to experience Japan at its best (and worst!)

Over the next week, Diane and I toured around Kyoto and I taught in her English class at school. Japan is a fascinating country, steeped in ancient traditions and rituals. If ever I was given the chance to explain this to my grandfather though, I don't think I could do it. He had his thoughts, experiences and memories; I'll have mine.

Upon my return home to a wintry UK, the doctors finally agreed to remove my appendix. I told them nothing of my adventures, but smiled politely and awaited surgery. The following spring I was admitted and had what the surgeon described as "the most inflamed appendix I've ever taken out during surgery". "You're a lucky man!"

CHAPTER 3 - MT FUJI

CHAPTER 4
MT KINABALU
BORNEO
OCTOBER 2005

*"When you're drowning, you don't say
'I would be incredibly pleased if someone
would have the foresight to notice me
drowning and come and help me,'
you just scream!"*

JOHN LENNON

Borneo, or to be more accurate, Sabah, was one hell of a change of scenery for my next challenge. I had moved from Arctic glaciers and a pumice strewn volcano to find myself in dense primary rainforest to climb my next peak, Mt Kinabalu. I had travelled to Asia many times before, indeed bashed through a good bit of its undergrowth in my time, so I felt quite happy in my surroundings. At home in the UK I had felt lost and didn't want to travel alone, so hopped on an Exodus trip to Borneo to give me a little company.

Thunderstorms lit the sky as the plane descended into the coastal town of Miri. I hoped it wasn't going to be a bad omen. The weather was wet to start my trip, but cleared the next morning to reveal burning sunshine.

I met the group in a smart and overpowering hotel before we set off for a lovely few days together touring the Mulu Caves (where we met a British Caving Expedition mapping out new caverns and potholes), walking the Headhunters Trail and generally wandering through the undergrowth.

The best way to get around this part of the world is by boat as roads are few, if not non-existent. Most settlements are close to water, so it made sense to hop on for rides here and there. I was having a whale of a time, chatting to new faces and sharing stories, when we split the group into three and jumped on a trio of riverboats. They are sleek, swift craft, fashioned from long planks of wood and powered by a single outboard motor. We sped down the Terikan River and watched kingfishers dance above the water with not a care in the world.

The river turned sharp right and entered a narrows with a little white water. It frothed in places, but looked unexciting and was nothing more than we had passed many times previously. The first boat went through smartly and the second boat (which I was on) soon followed. As we entered the rapids I felt the boat smack hard against a rock. The shudder ran through my spine. She began to roll clockwise, take in water and sank at high speed. Have you ever seen a film where action shots are shown in slow motion? That's exactly what the next few seconds felt like. Everyone began to fall out to the right, followed by kitbags, walking poles and associated gear. It felt like minutes, but in reality took only a few seconds. Before I knew it I was headfirst underwater being kicked and bashed by flailing limbs. I looked up to see the sunshine dazzle through the chaos, before the stern of the boat went over my head. The outboard was still going at breakneck speed and the prop missed me, by how much I'm not sure. I tried to swim to the surface, but everywhere there were arms, legs and bags hitting me. I punched through them, took half a breath, heard someone scream "Stop kicking!" and went underwater again. This dive felt deeper and I felt the dangerous hand of panic fall gently on my shoulder. I burst for the surface again, took another breath and was about to go down when a hand grabbed my shirt and dragged me skyward to safety.

The river was a mess. The boat handler had dragged the outboard onto a rock and was apologising profusely to everyone. The rapids were full of half-drowned people and the air was blue. I began to gather my thoughts and stood thigh deep on the now jammed craft as it sat pinned against the rocks and half submerged at 90°. As I stood on the gunnels, I helped to drag some of the bags ashore and generally took stock of the situation. People were half drowned but ok and stood up to their waists gathering themselves and their gear.

Suddenly I heard a loud scream. I looked upstream to be faced with the third boat appearing from round the bend and entering the rapids. It was heading straight for me and had no hope of stopping.

There was nowhere and no time to run. The face on the

first passenger was strewn with pure horror as she ploughed onward to drive over me. Another one of those slow motion moments was about to begin. Out of pure instinct I waited until the boat came close, leapt forward and grabbed its gunnels. I pushed with all my might and jammed it into my sunken boat. It hit hard, but held tight. I gripped with my battered hands for grim death and screamed at everyone in the water "GET OUT, NOW!" They scrambled for shore and dragged themselves out on their hands and knees onto the muddy bank. When they were safe I lifted the boat straight up out of the water, pushed with all my might and threw it to my left. It shot by as I guided the gunnels past my legs and safely downstream.

All the excitement was over. The first boat had landed and the passengers had recovered some of the bags as they floated by. It came back upstream and retrieved us from the rocks, depositing us in safety on the bank below. I watched as the Malays recovered the sunken boat and its wares to salvage what they could and carry out repairs. Water was pouring from every part of me and I had swallowed a fair bit too. My eyes were stinging, but at least I could see. Of all the gear, we only lost a couple of ski poles and miraculously no one was physically hurt.

If I hadn't seen the other boat in time, well I might not be writing these words now. If the boat had struck me full on I would have easily come away with broken legs or worse.

I had enough trouble over the next few days due to mouthfuls of river water working through my system, but they were the only physical symptoms. The nightmares that followed for the next week left me unhappy on the water for the rest of the trip.

My gear was soaked, my cameras trashed, my passport and travellers cheques left drying on the grass, but I was alive and thankful for it.

I bought new cameras in Kota Kinabalu and after a brief visit to the orang-utan centre at Sepilock, made for the real objective of my trip – Mt Kinabalu.

Before I go into the climb, I'd like to say something. On the road to Sepilock I passed mile after mile of desolation. When I say that, I don't mean ten or fifteen miles, I mean hundreds. The rainforest had been cut down for its hardwoods and palm oil plantations had been created in its wake. Palm oil may be useful for biofuels and food production, but I think we have to consider the environmental damage that creating this oil produces. If someone came to your house to chop it down for a crop, then you'd have something to say, but the animals can't talk, or indeed protest. We evict them as we wish, when we wish, to suit our own selfish needs. We have to stop treating the world like a plaything and understand what the hell we are doing to it! Right, rant over...

Standing at 4095 m (13,431 ft) high, Mt Kinabalu is the highest point between the Himalayas and New Guinea. She was first climbed in 1851 by Sir Hugh Low and has since become a very popular tourist attraction – around 30,000 people a year attempt to climb (well walk) up it, as it's one of the easiest peaks in the world to summit. It's a far cry from the wastelands of Baffin Island, but nevertheless, it's on the Seven Islands list.

After a soak in Poring Hot Springs we overnighted in the bustling town of Ranau. The air was filled with the sound of revving scooters and beeping car horns, quite the opposite of most places I stay to climb. The climate was cool and the evening air refreshing after the sticky heat of the jungle. The hotels and bars resembled some kind of holiday resort, but that's the effect we have on communities like this around the world. If someone discovers something wonderful, it's not a secret for long and the tourists soon pour in.

The next day dawned bright and warm. Swifts darted through the air outside my window and into their under-eaves nest. I grabbed my bag and joined the hundreds plodding up the well-worn path to the hut at Panar Laban. The route was simple enough, but the permits and politics were painfully slow to sort. Bureaucracy is the killer of many a good business, but when you hold the prize in your hand, you get to make the rules. After a very long and boring wait in the burning sun we set off at a steady pace, initially downhill, which felt completely wrong, but we were soon climbing. I noticed plenty of folk go belting off up the slope, but knew we had all day and decided to take my time. We would soon be at the edge of altitude and though the forest below provided extra oxygen, I could see no point in making myself ill. As Gandhi once said, "There is more to life than increasing its speed."

The hares soon began to flag and the tortoises caught them up. The steady plod was working well and the daylight was on our side. The wide, at times stepped path was easy going underfoot and had a wooden handrail in sections. The air became tight on the lungs, but nothing to talk about. By now I was carrying not only my own kit but also someone else's, whistling quietly to myself and thoroughly enjoying the day. One or two others were not and tempers began to fray, but there's no point in losing it. "Just put one foot in front of the other and take your time," I told them.

I must comment about the beautiful peak that Kinabalu is. It cuts a huge silhouette out of the jungle horizon and stands alone. The rock peaks that adorn her summit are spectacular, bare and like nothing around them. They catch the sun, particularly at both ends of the day, and glow crimson. She is the centrepiece of Kinabalu National Park and brings people from around the world to visit and climb her. The park is an oasis of nature, unfortunately now surrounded by man's damaging effects. Plantations, conurbations and roads interlace the lowlands. There are even masts on the peak's side, so is our insatiable desire for modern communications.

Of the seven shelters on the way up, I sat in every one, watched numerous nationalities argue about speed, time and height, and made it to the hut during mid afternoon. I had seen mountain ground squirrels, birds galore, bearded oak forests and even dandelions! It had been a beautiful walk. Outside the hut, a few locals played raga, a type of volleyball, but using only feet. Their acrobatics made enjoyable viewing. Some people just sat about, taking in the stunning views over the jungle below. The skies were clear and I used my rucksack as a pillow for forty winks. From inside the hut I could hear people complaining about headaches and breathlessness. Many were suffering from going too high to fast and dehydration wasn't helping. This is one of the great dangers of altitude. The attitudes of "well, it's only a few thousand feet high" or "I'm fit, no problem", mean little at height. Reality and truth do. Not just truth to yourself, but truth to others too. If you ache or hurt, tell someone. Soldiering on is all very British and stiff upper lip, but no good for your health. Kinabalu is, for many people, the highest they have been or will ever be. I think the profile of the mountain fools people into a false sense of security; after all, at this height in the Alps it would be glaciated and snowcapped.

Panar Laban is more like a three-storey prefab that an Alpine hut, but it serves an excellent purpose and provides simple food and somewhere to sleep. It was packed to the rafters that evening and buzzing.

Evening began to fall and the sun set. The lights of the towns below illuminated the night floor and the stars up above lit the night sky. The last rays of the sun dropped behind the horizon, and I went to bed – bag packed and kit ready. With a 3am start I wanted to be asleep early, but the population of the Panar Laban hut had other ideas. The wooden floors creaked and banged to dozens of running feet, the hallways were echoing with voices and in the background was a TV and Karaoke machine. I stuck my head under the covers and eventually managed to drop off...

At 2:15am the hut exploded into life. The sounds of rustling bags and clomping boots filled the air. Coats were donned and bootlaces tied in a fervour of activity and excitement. Wherever I climb, the excitement of summit day still stays with me. I walked down the creaky wooden stairs, out into the darkness below and awaited the group. Soon we were off, following a procession of head torches as they snaked up into the darkness. The air was still, the night cool and except for a few voices, the mountain was silent.

Believe it or not, there is a checkpoint which you have to cross, showing your mountain pass. This is where the queuing started again. I had awaited it at the base of the climb, and once again stood in line for my pass to be inspected. Many countries use their mountains as a source of income, particularly the Himalayan states. I have no problem with that, provided the cost is fair and the funds used to good effect. The latter is difficult to prove.

As we climbed, a few people began to fall by the wayside. I particularly note one group of Japanese tourists, who, like the man on Mt Fuji, were on aerosol oxygen. They had run out and were suffering. A hand grabbed my leg and a weak voice said, "Medicine, medicine!" "I don't have any, go down!" I replied, but it meant little to them. All I could do was keep going and leave them to their own choices. At a little over 10,000 ft, they should have descended immediately and given up, but that is not their way. I have seen friends suffer and collapse on the hill and it's an awful thing to watch. The best you can do is get them down immediately. If an oedema sets in, then you are in serious trouble.

The jungle at the base of Kinabalu was changing into tundra on its heights. Willow trees and rhododendron bushes took over until even they were replaced by bare granite. I felt confident and happy with the ascent and was suffering little to the effects of the altitude. Once again the sprinters were off to get the best seating spots for the dawn and I let them go. It would be cold up there and I much preferred to keep moving slowly, arriving in the nick of time if I could.

Across the granite was laid a thick white three-ply rope. It had been placed as a guide to the summit and as a safety line in case of ice on the rock, which does form occasionally. That I do understand, but what I don't is the necessity to hold onto it at ground level, fully bent over in a long procession and follow it. Sure enough there were dozens of people with their bums in the air, hanging on. Their heads were bloodshot and like a huge centipede they slowly followed each other's arses. If I hadn't seen this bizarre spectacle, I wouldn't have believed it. I just walked past them, perfectly upright and amazed at their position. The granite was dry and my boots felt glued onto it.

Silhouetted in the half light before me was Lows Peak. I scrambled up its broken boulder field and arrived at the summit around 5:30am. Surely enough, a few people had been there over half an hour and were complaining of the cold. The dawn looked clear and one by one the stars disappeared in the morning glow. Dawn broke at 5:45am. Deep red light flooded over us, illuminating Ugly Sister Peak and casting a pyramid shadow behind her. The sky changed slowly from deep red to dark blue to yellow as the sun sneaked over the horizon.

Below me sat miles of cloudy jungle, the South China Sea to the north-west, the Philippine Sea to the north-east and the city of Kota Kinabalu on the eastern coast. Lows Gulley sat directly under me and was lit with smoky stripes of sunlight which broke through the clouds of moist jungle air. Around me the buzz of a hundred people filled the atmosphere, but I was in my own world, if only for a few moments. "Four down, three to go," I thought. I unfurled my Union Flag for the customary photo and watched as people began to leave in droves. At high altitude where time is everything or the temperature bitter I can understand this, but it was a beautiful and warming day. Have we created a society which works on "done that, now I'm off"? I just enjoyed the views, particularly of Mt Trus Madi, standing to the south in the Crocker Range, as I was going to have a crack at her later in the week when everyone else had gone. The Kinabalu guides said, "Very beautiful, but full of mosquitoes!"

The commercial aspect of my trip was almost over and I was off to travel alone. Just as I was about to leave the summit, the Japanese party appeared below Lows Peak on their hands and knees and crawled to the top.

Descending allowed me to view the route in daylight and in particular the white rope. It made an excellent guide over the blank granite plateau, but I do wonder about its other uses. The thousands of steps down ground at my knees and I wished for snow and a pair of skis, but the seven islands are spread far and wide across the surface of the Earth. I dropped in for a spot of breakfast at the hut and six hours later walked slowly through the park gates and onto the road below. My feet were aching like hell. Losing your toes does nothing for your descent. You cannot feel what's before you, nor extend your foot well as the tendons that connected your calves to your feet are all over the place. Still, I have to accept my injuries for what they are and how they have changed my life.

The trip split up a few days later and 1 travelled south to climb Mt Trus Madi, Sabah's second highest peak. Though not on the Seven Islands circuit, it sounded fascinating and as 1 found out, was much quieter, remote and untouched than Kinabalu. It was strewn with rare pitcher plants, thick jungle, wildlife galore and gave excellent views of Mt Kinabalu. 1 even saw the rare Rafflesia in flower. To top it all my guide and 1 were caught in a lightning storm on the summit. I'd be surprised if thirty people a year climb Trus Madi and in case you are interested, there was hardly a mosquito in sight!

CHAPTER 5
GUNUNG KERINCI PT 1
SUMATRA
OCTOBER 2005

"Despair is the price one pays for setting oneself an impossible aim"

GRAHAM GREENE

Confusing title? Hopefully it will make sense by the end of this chapter...

After climbing Mt Trus Madi, I took a flight from Kota Kinabalu, through Kuala Lumpur and onto Padang in Sumatra. This was my second time to the island. I had travelled here years before and struggled with the "Hello Mr!" syndrome and didn't look forward to the battering to come. Really, it's very simple. Every child, and I mean every child, would shout "Hello Mr!" to you, regardless of your nationality or even sex. I found it irritating until I discovered that the youngster is only trying to be polite and use some English. Still, twenty times a minute does get a little wearing.

I left the airport in a taxi bound for Padang's main bus station, which for some bizarre reason is eight miles out of town. How can I even begin to describe this place? Let's try a large dusty yard with battered tin buildings on three sides. Though plenty of people stand around, no one seems to know what is going where, and as you argue about tickets and prices all you can smell is raw sewage. Your bags disappear, then reappear on different buses, so you move, then move again and again, wondering if you will ever see your kit again. The food stalls were covered in clouds of flies and I decided it was better to starve than eat. Does that give you some impression? I'm not trying to make the place sound more awful than it is, just reporting the truth.

When the bus does leave it circles town until it fills. This can take a couple of hours. Thankfully, having travelled here before I understood this, but as a first-timer it would be hard to take in.

Sumatran buses are beautifully painted and decorated. The half-inch of filler that covers them is immaculately sanded and prepared, before being covered in murals and names of the company, route or driver. City backstreets are full of garages working on half-stripped and beaten vehicles. The local rivers usually have a couple parked in the water – the local car wash. Mechanically they are probably a death trap, but you don't worry too much about that. If you did, well, you'd never get anywhere on the island. A couple of other things to note about Sumatran buses. On a less travelled route, you will be the centre of attention and people will want to talk to you, no matter how deep the base is as it booms through the bus. Also expect the roads of hell and thick black smoke from the exhaust as you climb. I'm not trying to put anyone off as Sumatra is a beautiful island, but it does have its challenges.

I boarded the bus to Sungaipenuh and held on as we left the suburbs of Padang and climbed into the mountains of the interior. I hoped my bags were on the roof.

For the next seven hours we bumped and slid along. The roads were firstly good tarmac, but soon disintegrated into stone, before returning to tarmac and then stone. You get the idea. The hairpin bends were interesting to say the least as the back of the bus (where I sat) seemed to overhang them. The scenery, however, was stunning – high pastures, paddy fields and tea plantations dotted with simple farms and houses. Gin clear lakes stood below huge scree faces. It was beautiful and mostly untouched. The tea plantations got more frequent due to the high rainfall and rich soils that are part of the Sumatran Highlands. We stopped in a few villages for breaks and to stretch our legs. In one the local school must have been emptying out for the day and the most immaculately dressed and presented children appeared in the street. They were polite and very interested in me. What amazed me was their dress – pressed blazers, smart trousers or skirts, shirts and ties. Their surroundings dictated otherwise, yet at home I hardly see a schoolchild tidy at all. Most have half their backside hanging out and don't talk, just grunt.

I entered Kerinci Seblat National Park without even noticing, but a kind passenger pointed out what I was after – Gunung Kerinci (3805 m). She was half covered in cloud, but the weather looked clear and I felt confident. Kerinci is an active volcano and bordered by rich tea plantations of the Kayo Aro estate. It stands on a high plateau and is alone in its altitude.

The bus entered the small, but strung-out village of Kersik Tua. I had informed the driver hours ago in Padang of my destination and he remembered exactly where I wanted to go, in fact he asked around and took me to the Homestay Subandi, where I was staying. He even knocked at the door and chatted to Mrs Subandi. Their language seemed agitated and I knew something was wrong. "You cannot go up," said Mrs Subandi. "Eruption, too much ash. My husband away until tomorrow. Come back then." My heart fell. There hadn't been a serious eruption since 1934, but seventy-one years later I had managed to find one. I was at a loss at what to do. I was stood in southern Sumatra with a bus full of people waiting on my decision. "Come to the park office in Sungaipenuh and talk to the ranger there," suggested the driver. I didn't know what else to do, so just hopped aboard for an extra hour down the hill.

Sungaipenuh didn't fill me with joy. It looked dirty and untravelled to the western eye. The streets were strewn with litter and the bus station resembled a madhouse. The sunlight was fading and I didn't fancy being alone here in the dark. Thankfully the bus driver knew a few people and after lots of talking he got me in at a local guesthouse. It was a bit of a dump, grubby and dimly lit, but it was cheap and had a roof and a bed.

I needed to eat and found a small corner cafe which

sold decent rice. The worry was that a man was following me, wanting to try his English. I wasn't really in the mood, but he sat opposite me and talked incessantly. I was polite, but really wanted some peace and quiet to think. I was halfway around the world in a town I didn't know, feeling quite lost about a peak I couldn't climb. It came to a head when he asked me to explain, "What does it mean Never Mind the Bollocks?" I have to say that I wasn't expecting that. I did my best, but hardly succeeded in a true explanation. The phrase is one thing, but the Sex Pistols were something else! He invited me to his home, I declined, wished him goodnight and locked myself in my hotel room.

The next morning I felt a little better, but itched to find out what was going on high up on Kerinci. I struggled to find the National Parks Office, so did what you should always do – ask a policeman. A young lad of 21 in full uniform fired up his scooter and said, "I'll take you there now if you like." We sped through the dusty morning streets at breakneck speed and there appeared a beautifully adorned, but firmly locked closed Parks Office. The policeman didn't think they would open that day as Ramadan was in full swing. So then, now what could I do? What felt like a hopeless situation was saved when the policeman said, "Let's get your bags and I'll get you on a bus to Kersik Tua. You will be able to find out more there." It might not have been correct enforcement protocol, but within minutes I was sitting on the pillion seat of the scooter with my kitbag across my knees! The lad seemed to be having a whale of a time scurrying in between carts, cars, sleeping dogs and whatever else was in the road at the time. His English was excellent and I was very lucky and very glad that I found him. Sure enough he put me on the bus back up the hill and waved me goodbye.

An hour later I knocked on the door of Homestay Subandi

and met the man I had been looking for – Pak Subandi. He is a local environmentalist, bird watcher and legend. What he doesn't know about the area isn't worth knowing. We sat down with some tea and he explained that a great deal of ash was spewing from Kerinci and falling in the jungles around. Large clouds of carbon monoxide gas and sulphur were also filling the slopes, making climbing impossible. Well, that stopped me in my tracks, but at least I knew. So what to do? My flights home were fixed so I stayed a few days and met one of Pak's guides called En. We did a little jungle bashing and had a day's walk to Lake Gunung Tujuh, which is the highest volcanic lake in SE Asia, before I wished them goodbye and took the seven-hour journey back to Padang. After a brief visit to Bukittinggi and Lake Maninjau I flew westward and returned home.

The trip hadn't been what I hoped, but it taught me valuable lessons about the Seven Islands challenge and about life itself. We cannot always expect things to go our way all of the time. Nature, people, car engines all have their funny ways and occasionally we have to accept the inevitable and get on with life. At least now I knew what to expect and who to call for my return.

CHAPTER 6
GUNUNG KERINCI PT 2
SUMATRA
OCTOBER 2006

"Today is your day! Your mountain is waiting. So... get on your way"

DR SEUSS

The boss was talking to someone, about something unimportant – to me anyway. What I thought important was to find out if Gunung Kerinci was clear of eruptions and to see if I could climb her. I sneaked out of the office armed with my mobile phone and Lonely Planet guide to Indonesia. I found a quiet corner and dialled Pak Subandi in Kersik Tua. After only a few moments he answered over a surprisingly clear line and told me what I wanted to hear: "The eruptions have stopped and you should come as soon as you can.

Once again I found myself on the seven-hour journey to Kersik Tua, but this time I wasn't in a bus. There had been an almighty cock up in Padang Airport and I had ended up sitting in a travel agent's office awaiting a taxi. The buses were full for the next three days (apparently). This isn't too uncommon in Sumatra. It was Ramadan though and many people were travelling home to their families to celebrate. If the bus was full then a taxi could be found, but would only leave when it had been filled to braking point with people and their baggage. The backstreets of Padang were their uninspiring and dusty usual self as I sat outside the office awaiting my ride. Hours seemed to pass and every time I asked what was going on, no one seemed interested. Scooters and cars darted up and down the road, and in the river groups of teenagers were busily washing cars. I thought of Tina back at home waiting for me. How I would have loved to bring her here, but Sumatra was hard on your travel legs and she didn't have the time anyway. We had met years ago at work, but only recently got together. Again I found myself on the other side of the world and pining.

"Hey Mr, Mr! Your car is here!" a voice shouted from inside as a saloon pulled up. Along with four others I was packed inside and sent into the hills. I was charged only bus fare, which seemed very reasonable, and even given the front seat. It was late afternoon when we left the suburbs in heavy rain and soon darkness enveloped us.

I remembered part of the journey, but in the blackness of the night it was difficult to make much out. There were no streetlights and the moon was hidden by cloud. We stopped at the same rest stops (I think), and dropped everyone but myself off before climbing high into the mountains. I had dozed on and off for the journey due to jetlag, but began to recognise the entrance to Kersik Tua. I tried to tell the driver where to stop, but he kept going and turned up a long field track. We drove for a few hundred yards and suddenly stopped. There was a click and the passenger side back door opened. At huge bloke clad in camouflage fatigues and wearing a pistol got in, closed the door and said something to the driver. We slowly pulled off into the night. I hardly dared look round at the character behind me and began to shake. The night was cool, but beads of sweat began to run down my spine. "Who was this bloke? Where did he come from? Why was he in the car? Why was he armed?" I feared for my life and fully expected to be found face down by the roadside with a bullet in the back of my head. He started to talk with the driver, but an argument soon began.

After a few minutes cruising around I had to say something. I wasn't quite sure what was going to happen, but if I was going to die, well I might as well fight for myself. I had struggled with argument and confrontation all my life, but I looked across at the driver and kept repeating "Subandi" louder and louder. The man in the back started to shout and the brakes went on. The other back door opened and a young boy jumped in. Arms flew everywhere, voices were raised and fingers pointed as the driver nervously turned right and left down tracks and almost over fields. I made out the shadow of tea bushes and hedges, but little more before we stopped and the driver pointed across me. "Subandi!" he said, rather aggravated. We were outside the Homestay Subandi and at the door stood Pak. "Thank God for that," I murmured, grabbed my bags and walked in. The young lad was a local and had guided us to Mr Subandi, but I never knew who the armed man was. The taxi disappeared into the darkness and thankfully I never saw it again. Relief was not the word!

Inside Pak's house the mood was light, the food excellent and the bed soft (by Sumatran standards anyway). Gunung Kerinci was clear to climb and the guide that I met last year would be joining me. The weather had been stormy as of late with hailstorms and rain, but the forecast was for it to clear. I rang Tina, but couldn't face telling her what I had been through. She worried about me enough already and I couldn't blame her for that. I blew out the candle and slept like a log after one hell of a day's travelling.

The next morning things looked a little clearer, in my head anyway. Outside there was thick fog. Not from the usual moisture clouds as you may think, but from commercial logging miles away. The smoke from the brush fires mixes with the natural clouds and creates a thick mist over the hills. There was no smell of burning though.

En joined me after breakfast with his beaming smile and strong handshake. He was delighted to see "Mr John" again. Let me explain. Nigel is sometimes a difficult name to pronounce in parts of the world. 'G' is said as a 'J', 'I' as 'E', etc. My middle name is John and I have been called Juan and Jean before, depending on country or continent. It doesn't bother me at all as I can't see the point in making life hard for other people. I hope that makes sense?

The breeze cleared a little of the fog and Kerinci stood out like a ghost. Being a volcano, there was nothing around her, no ridges and no range. Like Mt Fuji she stands tall, conical and alone. En called a couple of friends with scooters over (one for each of us), and we sped down the plantation road towards the trailhead. The wind blasted into my face and I felt alive. At last, after so much travelling and effort I was going to get my chance. The road was bumpy and undulating, but hilarious fun. I thought a couple of times we were going for a dive, but we stayed upright and within a few minutes were waving the riders away as they left. Their two-stroke engines disappeared into the distance and silence reigned. I turned, walked through the last of the tea plantation and straight into the rainforest.

The lower slopes were thick in trees, bushes, ferns, vines and creepers. The path was well worn, however, and simple enough to follow. People had walked here since the Dutch colonial days; indeed there had been stations and even a telephone line at some point, En informed me. The air felt rich with oxygen. It felt almost primeval and untouched by man. The floor was not though as I soon began to see plastic bottles and packets strewn over the ground. My heart fell. What makes people think they have the right to drop crap everywhere they go? The human race can be the most wonderful thing in the world and also the most self-centred and disgusting. I have always worked on the principle that we are the visitors and guests that nature allows. We don't own anything and we can't buy everything. Talking of which, we also came across areas where mature hardwoods had been felled, stripped and stolen from the National Park. Whilst some say that this is acceptable and keeps the market demand away from other areas, I cannot agree. The damage done and devastation left are too much in such a beautiful area.

My rucksack caught on the undergrowth again and again as the path narrowed. Over the years, torrents of rain had cut narrow trenches through the soil, which we had to force our way up. I struggled to tear my bag free of the spiky creepers without injury and my face, arms and hands were scratched to pieces. A scratch here can easily get infected and turn nasty, but I sat later and cleaned myself up with antiseptic.

En unpacked lunch and we sat talking about lives. I noticed that he wasn't eating, and then realised what I was doing. It was Ramadan and En was not allowed to eat until sunset. Or smoke or drink come to that. I felt incredibly guilty, but he didn't mind at all. We both understood our different perspectives on religion. I was Church of England, he Muslim. It wasn't a problem to either of us. I find the travelling environment a pretty innocent one as few people complain about others' ways of life. It seems the press at home feel otherwise, but as I have mentioned before, we have no right to press our thoughts and demands onto others. En disappeared for a few minutes to quietly pray, before we picked up our bags and continued ascending.

Below us I heard a clatter in the jungle. A party of four Czech climbers were smashing their way up the hill, shouting, whistling and generally frightening every bit of wildlife away for miles. They were polite enough, said hello and smiled as they overtook us at great speed. About half an hour later the birds, monkeys and lizards we had seen earlier returned.

My recent flights and jetlag were beginning to take their toll. I was still six hours behind Sumatran time and starting to flag. I had been on my feet for nine hours with a packed 60 litre bag on my back and was relieved when En said we were at the campsite. The only piece of flat ground for miles was the remains of an old Dutch hut at 3000 m (9800 ft). A metal skeleton with a sandy floor was all that was left and I pitched my tent between the rusty metal posts. We built a tarp shelter under which to cook and sat under the stars. High altitude, clear skies and the lack of light pollution allowed them to shine in their thousands. The Milky Way was visible across the sky and shooting stars burst into stripes of light. The night was cold and we donned hats and coats to ward off the freezing temperatures.

En was relieved to drink, eat and have a fag. His face relaxed tremendously at the taste of tobacco. After every drag he blew the smoke out slowly to enjoy every last molecule of nicotine.

We began to talk about life and I had some trouble explaining to En that Tina was my girlfriend, so resorted to saying that she was my wife. This might sound strange to western eyes, but to En it made perfect sense. No offence was intended and hopefully none was taken by either party. We just have to understand other people's points of view of how life should be lived.

After a couple of hours my eyelids took a decision and forced me into my bag.

I slept a few fitful hours, before my alarm sounded at 3:30am. My eyes were heavy, but it was time to get out into the cold night and head for the summit. As I dressed, the tent lining illuminated to the flickering yellow flames of En's stove. The light died in a few moments as the stove roared blue fire. After tea and biscuits we began our ascent by torch and star light. It was jet black, but cool and still.

The path narrowed again into knee-depth trenches. Their smooth sides gave little grip and in the darkness it was difficult to see what you were grabbing onto. The plants began to get shorter and stunted willows took over from tall trees. Ash fields ran between the smaller patches of vegetation until every living thing was gone and we were confronted by a dimly lit moonscape. Actually in the dim red light, it was probably more like Mars, but I'm not going to quibble over the relative surfaces of the solar system and its planets. We passed through the thin layers of clouds to be stood in the heavens and looked up towards space. In the distance the first tinges of blue were starting to warm the horizon and within minutes a red glow was rising. We were short of the summit, but facing due east without hindrance. I continued uphill, sliding on the dry dust that made up the summit. Behind me lay a trail of distinct boot prints in the talc-like ash. You could not hide your tracks here, but always had a clear path home.

The sun rose quickly, casting a deep red glow across the ash fields, which changed to bright orange and ash grey in minutes. The air grew suddenly warmer and more inviting, giving me a boost of energy for the top. My lungs filled with sulphurous air and my ears picked up a dim rumble. I was almost there.

Within minutes I had walked over a rise and from the narrow rim I stared across the mile-wide crater of Kerinci. Five down, two to go. En turned and said, "Welcome to the top, John; highest point in Sumatra 3805!" We shook hands and relief ran through my bones. I had managed it the second time and could now cast away the stresses of my journey, for now anyway. It was 6:30am and the sun was casting misty shadows into the chasm below. The sulphur was almost overpowering and the rumble had become a roar. Below me lay a gaping hole half a mile deep. In its depths a pool of boiling sulphur was bubbling and steaming happily.

Around me sat a solid base of cloud, which obscured the jungle but reflected the power of the sun. It was becoming a beautiful day. I proudly raised my Union Flag as En took my picture. In the few days we had known each other, we had become good friends. Half an hour later the Czechs arrived en masse. We had passed their lonely tent earlier on an exposed section of ash. Apparently they had suffered a cold and windswept night with little sleep, but they looked fresh enough to me. We milled around taking pictures and I noticed them wandering a bit too close to the edge for my liking. I asked En what he thought. Apparently a Swiss team had once ventured too close and all six of them disappeared. They were never found. Lesson enough. The crater had been circumnavigated once or twice, but it was not for me. I was happy with my lot.

Technically the climb had been simple, with only a few roots and mud banks to negotiate, but that does not mean it is easy. People had got lost before high on the volcano and spent extra nights on the ash fields suffering exposure. The tropics are not always tropical.

It was time to descend to camp and head home. Following our tracks down through the ash fields was simple enough, but some of the trenches and gullies demanded careful negotiation to prevent a bum sliding luge run. We struck camp and quietly walked through the trees. I was glad of some shade as the sun had become overpowering in the open. En was not only a mountain guide, but also a keen birdwatcher and environmentalist. We talked quietly about the problems we all faced in the world, when something landed on the floor before me. "John, quick. Look!" He pointed high into the canopy, but I couldn't see a thing. Then something moved high up and swung on a long, leafy branch. We hid under a bush and sat quietly. I eased the telephoto lens from my camera case, wincing with every tear of the Velcro strap. "What's going on?" I whispered, but En said nothing. He pointed at one shadow in hundreds of others. Then there was a crash and branches twanged and shattered. "Black gibbons," whispered En. He opened a pair of old brass binoculars and took a long, slow look at them. About a dozen were on the canopy top, perhaps forty feet up. They had thrown some fruit at me as a warning, but as we hid, they calmed down. As silently as we could, we followed them through the forest and I tried to take a few photos. They were incredibly fast through the trees, but gave a beautiful finale to my Kerinci adventure.

Suddenly fruit began to fly down in huge quantities. It was like a hailstorm. I couldn't imagine we had got so close to be a threat, but then realised what was aggravating them. The Czechs were coming with their usual delicate crashing and conversations. Within seconds the gibbons were gone.

We climbed Gunung Kerinci so fast that I still had jetlag when we returned to Kersik Tua. I slept when I could and called Tina down a crackly phone line. We had been apart less than a week, but were missing each other terribly. Her voice may have been distant, but it made my heart miss a beat. It would be over three weeks before I returned home and I wondered how we would manage. We would, we had to.

There was time to spare before my flight out from Padang to Jakarta, so I spent three days with En searching for the illusive Sumatran tiger. We hacked through remote jungle filled with orchids, deer, hornbills and leeches, but alas, no tigers.

Time to head for Jakarta...

CHAPTER 7
CARSTENSZ PYRAMID
IRIAN JAYA
OCTOBER 2006

"A friend is someone who understands your past, believes in your future and accepts you just the way you are"

UNKNOWN

I flew into the sprawling capital of Indonesia as evening fell. I wasn't sure if the ghostly haze hanging over the city was cloud or pollution until I walked onto the tarmac and coughed. I grabbed my bags and was met by Harry, a very excited young man who was to be my guide for the next day or so. He was tall, slim and had a beaming smile with pearly white teeth. The temperature difference between Gunung Kerinci and Jakarta was incredible, as was the humidity. My back soon ran with sweat as we fought our way through the city to meet the other climbers in the party. The motorway was solid with traffic and our minibus driver thought himself on the RAC rally!

I had booked with Adventure Peaks from the Lake District for the assault on Carstensz Pyramid and had instructions to meet everyone in the Kaiser Hotel that evening.

There are times in your life when mistakes can be easily made. I was introduced to an Indian climber called Sibu. He firmly shook my hand and announced that he was an IT consultant from Delhi who was soloing the Seven Summits. He seemed a little gruff, over formal and uninterested in anyone around him. I was polite enough and said hello before being whisked away to my room. Here I met Dave Pritt, the expedition leader. Dave was a Lakeland lad, brought up in the fells and an excellent mountain guide. He ran Adventure Peaks and had never climbed in Irian Jaya, so had decided to personally come and face the mountain. He was shattered and soon sleeping after the long flight from the UK, so I left him to it and went downstairs to find Sibu. Now the fun started...

A tall South African was introduced to me. His name was Sibu. "There can't be two of them," I thought. "Peter, yes, Paul, perhaps, but Sibu?" Here was the case of mistaken identity. Indeed I was before Sibu, the half Zulu, half Swazi game ranger and Everest summiter with his beaming smile, loud laugh and welcoming attitude. He was quite a different person from the Indian chap (who I later found was called Malli) I had been introduced to earlier. Before I knew it we were chatting like old friends over dinner and swapping stories. He was intrigued by my epic on McKinley and I listened intently at his near-death climb on Everest's North Side. He was convinced that we had met before, but I could not recall it. In 1992 I had been climbing in Nepal and during an acclimatisation day on Pokalde I met a group who were going to climb Mera Peak. They seemed well charged up for the challenge, but that was all I could recall. Sibu had been with them. He remembered my hands and had asked the leader about me. The funny thing was that the leader climbed at the same wall in Nottingham that I did. Strange thing this world of ours...

Before we get too buried in all that, I should mention that this was an international team also encompassing both Japanese and Indian climbers. I feel that I must mention that everyone but myself had summited Everest, along with numerous other high peaks, and were heavily sponsored (one had received £37,000 for this trip alone!). It was easy to be overcome with their tales and stories as there I was, a simple Derbyshire lad having to pay his own way. Terra Nova of Alfreton has supported me on many expeditions, and Nottingham Climbing Wall help too, but expedition money has to come from my own pocket. Every year it gets harder to find, but enough about all that. We had a mountain to climb...

I had a brief few moments with Tina on the telephone before we set off for Carstensz. We hardly knew what to say, but knew exactly what we meant even though we were thousands of miles apart. I gently placed the receiver down, let out a long breath and paid my bill, before walking to the bus for the airport.

Flying is the only real way to get across the huge archipelago that is Indonesia. From Jakarta, we flew four hours east to the island of Biak, before transferring to a twin otter for the final leg (for the day anyway) into Nabire on the north coast of Irian Jaya. I've lost count how many times I've flown in a twin otter. They might be ageing and basic, but are still the backbone of many countries' air fleets. At least I could get a look at what was below me as we flew low over the islands and reefs. The seas were deep blue, interspersed with small islands and coral. For some an idyllic paradise, but not for me. My heart is in the hills, not on the beach.

The journey was beginning to wear a few folk down. I was lucky having been in Indonesia for a week or two, but eyes were tiring as we sat before the sunset eating freshly cooked fish in a small shanty restaurant. Everything was good with the world except the TV in the corner. Even when silent they distract conversation, particularly when Shania Twain videos are being played!

The next step was the crucial one. We had to take an early morning flight to Enarotali, high in the hinterland of the island, before we learned about the fated helicopter ride. Carstensz Pyramid is located deep in the mountains and surrounded by dense jungle. A helicopter flight at high altitude is one of the only ways in, but the weather is fickle and soon grounds any attempt to travel. I had heard stories of folk waiting for days to get in and indeed out again and there had already been arguments between Dave and the locals over a number of issues, including travel. The jungle top flight to Enarotali was charged with excitement as we whizzed over the foothills and lakes before a dive-bomber approach and touch down into near havoc.

Misunderstanding a situation can be disastrous. Before the plane had even stopped the luggage hatch was open and kitbags were falling out. Hands grabbed at them madly and began to take them away. As a westerner your first thoughts are of theft. You want to leap out of the aircraft and scream at someone, knowing full well that they will hardly understand a word you are talking about. The locals were just being helpful and had no intent at all of stealing anything. They were just happy and rather intrigued at our clothing, electronic gadgets and sunglasses. It is here that friends and enemies alike can be made in seconds.

The dusty streets of Enarotali were quiet, wide and sun bleached. The buildings were simple, well spaced, clean and filled with smiling inhabitants. Our procession made it to the helipad in a few minutes and sat on the stony floor. The pungent smell of tarmac filed the air as part was being surfaced for the first time. Around us stood tall, undulating hills thickly wooded or faced with cliffs. It was peaceful and warm in the morning sun, so much so that I dozed on my kitbags. The rest didn't last long...

A crowd began to gather. The amount of Gore-Tex soon made it obvious that these were climbers joining the queue for the fabled helicopter. They looked a little worn, but were ecstatic at the news that today was to be a flying day. Some had been waiting here a week! We had been here 20 minutes. Patience is a virtue in the climbing world as much as anywhere else. Days at camp, stuck in awful conditions are not uncommon as Baffin had taught me, and getting lost in argument and stress does little to improve matters.

Due to sheer weight of numbers and amounts of gear to transport, we would need numerous hauls up the hill. It's 40 minutes each way plus refuel time for the chopper and pilot. He seemed insistent that a cup of steaming coffee be in his hand at all times and always had a cigarette burning. He introduced himself in perfect English and chatted quite socially before bursting into Indonesian at the ground crews. I say Indonesian, but many of the islands here have local languages and dialects. The Dani tribe, which inhabit this area, are an ancient race that until recently still lived in the stone age. Their traditions have survived, but it must have been one heck of a shock to go from stone to silicon in only a few years.

The first flight departed in a plume of dust and sand. I stood trying to get a shot with my video camera until the downdraft blew me over and spent the next 20 minutes cleaning dust off the lens. The booming rotors slipped into the silence before returning over an hour and a half later. I had been dozing again when the call came to get on board and go. Dave, Sibu and Malli had gone with the first lift, leaving myself and the Japanese climber Kyoushu Kurisan. His English was poor, but we got on well enough with gestures and smiles.

The film Apocalypse Now has a lot to answer for. When confronted with a Huey helicopter, the urge is to sit on the side with the door open, playing Wagner at high volume. This might be acceptable in Hollywood, but not in Irian Jaya. My requests to even have the door open were denied, due to the heights we would be flying at, and air regulations. Spoilsports...

The rotors burst into life and we were off. Firstly over cultivated fields before nature took over and smothered the land in trees, cliffs and waterfalls. Not a soul exists here and nature is allowed to do what nature does best – survive without our intervention. I say no one is here...

At the base of the range sits the Freeport Mine, a huge hole in the earth to extract copper, gold, silver and nickel from the rich soil and rock below. It is one of the largest man-made holes on the planet and visible from space. Sixty-ton trucks look like pinheads as they drive the spiral road into the mine.

Our world may need these metals, but should nature pay such a price? Millions of tons had been dug out and dumped onto the surrounding forest, destroying plants and animals alike. I'm not a politician and not going to get involved here, but just think what we do to the world to put that ring on your finger, or a chain around your neck.

The helicopter slipped over a cliff face and entered a narrow valley before swinging suddenly right. Below us I saw a small cluster of tents. It was base camp. Nestling against a small glacial lake and dominated by Carstensz herself, it was to be home for the next few days. We touched down in a flurry of dust and were beckoned outside with frantic hand gestures. I grabbed my bags and leapt onto the ground, suddenly feeling a shortness of breath. We had been transported from sea level to around 3600 m (12,000 ft) in a very short time and the altitude was biting. I felt better than most due to climbing Gunung Kerinci a week or so earlier, but it still stung. Four people suddenly ran past me with their heads down and leapt through the door. It was slammed shut and the chopper engines opened up. She left in a huge blast with condensation pouring off her rotors.

So we were there. Safe and at camp after a very short and lucky journey. All we had to do now was climb the beast, and she really looked a monster. The north face looked bare and daunting with the rock a deep battleship grey. The summit ridge was a dragon's back of pinnacles and towers, which sat silhouetted against the bright blue sky. I had sat below many such places in my past, wondering if I could do it and wondering how my injuries would cope. It was no use worrying. I was here and that would have to do.

The camp seemed like the last outpost of man. There was nothing after us for miles, but that didn't excuse certain aspects (in my view anyway) of what was going on. Any mountain camp will create waste; it's the way that we deal with it that matters. A large dome tent had been erected as a mess/dining room. Against it was a tarpaulin kitchen where excellent meals appeared. The problem was the piles of cans, packets and boxes stacked behind them. They were not bagged or tied down in any way and I knew exactly what the first gust of wind would do. People seemed a little uninterested, but I was assured that everything would be cleared away by the end of the climbing season. I had to trust them on that point.

Kurisan joined us later for a hot drink and a chat. He was pitched on the shoreline in a yellow two-man tent overhung with a huge solar panel to charge his myriad of gadgets and cameras. Somehow (and I don't know how) Sibu convinced him that the glacial lake had dangerous snakes in it. "They will come out of the water and get you!" he screamed excitedly. I still don't know if Kurisan really believed him, but for the rest of the trip, the buzzword was "Anaconda!" Words on a page don't allow me to share the actual sounds, but imagine an excited Japanese climber in almost Samurai style shouting "Anaconda!" on a regular basis.

If I'm going to be correct, the peak should be called Puncak Jaya, but was named Carstensz Pyramid after the Dutch explorer Jan Carstensz. He noticed glaciers on the range in 1623 and was ridiculed in Europe, as no one believed that ice could exist so close to the equator. Though the base was reached in the early part of the 20th century, it wasn't climbed until 1962 by a team lead by Heinrich Harrer.

Over the next day or so we reconnoitred the route and allowed our bodies to acclimatise further. Besides sharing a tent with Sibu, I began a great friendship with him. We sat and talked for hours. He had a family at home, and a large one

Summit of Gunung Kerinci

Carstensz Pyramid

Summit of Maramokoto

Kara - The best and most inspiring place to write there is...

at that. Leaving them was heartbreaking, but his adventures gave him a good income in South Africa, what with writing and speaking, and he felt a responsibility to provide for them. I talked of Tina a great deal and how I was missing her. I have always found it unusual how comparative strangers will open up and talk about themselves in a way that they would not do with good friends. Is it the fact that they fear no retribution or embarrassment, knowing that the other person is oblivious to their background? Who knows?

The next day was set as our summit attempt, so it was early to bed for a restless night.

The night drew on and on. Not because I was full of energy, in fact quite the opposite, but because of the weather. Rain began to fall and the clouds rolled in. There was no chance of an attempt in those conditions. "If I fail here, then it's over," I thought. The trip had cost me a huge amount of money and the chances of affording it again were tiny. This was my one and only chance.

At 3am my alarm sounded. I had slept for perhaps an hour and should have been shattered, but the adrenalin was flowing and that would have to keep me going for the next day. I thought back to similar situations in my past and remembered that I had once run on pure adrenalin for eleven weeks (before collapsing!). I was much younger then and without injury.

I stuck my head out of the tent – the rain had stopped earlier and the sky was clearing. Dave shouted over, "It looks ok, let's get going." Alpine starts are always a little chaotic. You know that you should eat, but it's early. You should go to the toilet, but it's early. My insides were shattered from the medication I had taken during my frostbite injuries and gave me trouble, day in, day out. Today was to be no exception.

Sibu, Dave and I set off into the darkness and plodded

silently up the screes. Our head torches punched holes through the blackness, but the ground was hard to make out and I slipped repeatedly on the loose rocks. Trail finding became a nightmare and we lost an hour as we struggled to find the fixed ropes at the start of the route. The incessant ups and downs of route finding through the scree fields began to grind at my heels. I cursed again and again under my breath as I felt sore patches appearing already. My heels were covered in protective tape, but the skin grafts were unhappy. It was going to be a long, painful day...

Eventually we clipped on and began our ascent. The first sections were climbed quickly due their relative ease and we moved well together. Behind me the dawn was breaking and shadows cast across the surrounding peaks and glaciers. The valley rain had turned into mountain snow bringing a strange feel to this tropical island.

The limestone was sharp and cutting, unlike the rock in my native Derbyshire, which had been worn smooth by thousands of climbers. After two hours of hard work we pulled up onto the summit ridge and took a break. So far, so good. The route was going better than I thought.

The sun burst onto the scene and within minutes the valleys were full of cloud. Above them on the ridge we warmed up and continued across the open and shattered rocks at a good pace. I was wondering what all the excitement about Carstensz Pyramid was. Had people just been winding us up? This seemed no harder than a Lakeland scramble. You know those moments in your life when you wish you had kept your mouth shut? Within minutes we were confronted by a blank rock face about thirty feet high. Down it ran a thick black rope, which we had to jumar up. A challenge enough indeed at altitude, but also a log jam as only one person can climb it.

Dave went first, giving out huge gasps and grunts as he fought upward. I followed. Fighting against gravity on foot can hurt enough, but on jumars it becomes another challenge. I spun round on the rope and bashed my helmet against the rock time and again. I would rest, get a couple of breaths and then with what felt like a Herculean effort, throw myself upward another few inches. I struggled to hold onto the jumar handle as my stubby fingers were tiring, but pushed onto the top after 10 minutes or so. My mouth was dry from a combination of panting, excitement and fear. I was shattered and sat down whilst Sibu almost flew up the rope. Thankfully we laughed at the top before moving on. Our comradeship threw away any thoughts of argument or distain. We were almost like brothers. A gap then appeared in the ridge. It was flanked on both sides by drops that disappeared into the clouds below. I abseiled into it, but could feel my vertigo beginning to bite and bite hard. I was thankful for the blanking effect of the cloud as it hid what must have been a huge drop below me as I jumped across the six feet or so of gaping chasm, before climbing up the other side to safety. Vertigo has been a part of my life for as long as I can remember and I have struggled to control it, but control it I must in places like this. We crossed another such gap a little further on, before a long slope opened up towards the thickening clouds. Visibility was fading fast...

At 11am I walked the last few steps onto the summit. I was standing on the highest point in SE Asia at 4884 m (16,024 ft) and couldn't see more than a few yards. Well, that's the weather for you. Mt Fuji had been similar, but at least I knew that the climbing was done. All I had to do was get down in one piece. Dave, Sibu and I shook hands and took the usual plethora of summit photos, all with a light grey backdrop. The summit was a little nondescript, but marked with the remains of flags from

Japan, Australia, the USA and home. A rusty tin contained a summit book, which we all signed, before I unfurled my Union Flag for a photo. Six down, only one to go.

Inside, a great weight lifted from my shoulders. I had put financial and time pressures on myself to come here and was scared stiff that I might fail. Fortunately for me, I hadn't, but luck had played its part. I sat my video camera on a rock and recorded a short message to Tina, knowing she would see me again before I could play it to her, but I didn't care.

It had taken eight hours to climb this far and we knew that the weather and time were not on our side. More cloud was rolling in and hail began to fall. It was time to head down to camp. You rarely get much time on a mountain's summit, but those precious minutes can stay with you all your life.

The hail turned into rain as we descended, soaking me and the ropes. My figure of eight grabbed repeatedly as I tried to abseil home and poured dirty grey water down my arms. A freezing wind got up and my hands began to fail me. My gloves sponged up the pouring water and began to freeze onto my skin. Losing the ability to grip when descending a steep, loose and exposed slope isn't funny at all and I had to stop on a couple of ledges to warm my damaged fingers up. There was no fear of frostbite again, but I have found that they close down and hibernate during intense cold. For the next day or so they would ache, but recover ok.

The rain got worse, creating streams and waterfalls down the gullies. I was abseiling up to my knees in water at one point and had to keep concentrating on the job in hand. It was easy to get distracted and that could mean a fall – not even worth contemplating in a place like this. An hour later I unclipped from the final rope and walked off the peak. My hands were scarred and my heels burning, but I was safe and only had the walk back to camp to contemplate. Dave and Sibu had climbed at lightning pace, but waited for me patiently and helped where they could. I was thankful for that. I'm by no means as fast as I was and do worry at what other people think of me.

I walked into camp 13 hours after I left and was met with hot food and drink. It's moments like these which will stick in my mind forever. So many people want this and that, demand more and think life is easy. Well it isn't. The blessed relief of a meal and drink meant more to me at that moment than possessions and money. We can live without both of them, but in the western world we choose not to. Will it be our undoing?

I slept like the dead that night, expecting a long lie in the next morning. I thought I was dreaming when I heard the radio burst into life across camp. Thinking nothing of it, I rolled over and tried to go back to sleep. "Guys, the chopper will be here in 20 minutes. Get packed up quick!" I'm a bit of a stickler when it comes to packing and organising, but there was no time for that. Sibu and I leapt and kicked sleeping bags, coats and gear into our kitbags, before knocking the tent down. We were fed a cuppa as the chaos progressed, but I wondered what the heck was going on. The weather was fine and the helicopter was flying, that's what was going on! Climbers were on their way up and we had to go. As the last poles of the tent were stuffed into their bags I heard the rotors coming. "Come on! Come on!" shouted Dave as we ran the best we could up to the helipad. With seconds to spare we sat down on the gear as the helicopter began its approach. It landed, spilled out three American climbers and sucked us on board. Within seconds we were airborne and away. It all seemed like some kind of military operation.

The 40-minute flight home was obstructed by cloud, but I wasn't really worried about the view. I was tired, hungry and bedraggled. We left the mountains behind and crossed the final plains into Enarotali. The pilot placed us gently down and stopped the engine. Peace reigned once more.

Our gear came out and another three Americans began to load up. They were the second group of a team of six, but it soon became apparent that they were going nowhere. The cloud we had flown home through was too thick for a return journey. I saw their faces drop at the news and again, realised how lucky we had been.

The pilot got his usual cup of coffee and had a cigarette on the go. There was much talk between him and some officials before he announced that he was heading down to Nabire and would give us a lift. This was a journey not to be missed!

At treetop height we crossed the jungle – it was Apocalypse Now again. I still had no luck with my request to get the side door open. We landed on a wooden helipad under blazing sun against the coast and began to boil. We had started our journey only an hour or two before dressed in fleeces and coats and were suddenly deposited in 40 °C. We stripped off in moments, fighting through awfully packed bags for shorts and t-shirts. By the time evening fell I was sitting on a beach with a tall drink, watching the sunset. It was a day of huge contrasts.

The question now was what to do? We had thought that Carstensz Pyramid would take a week to climb and then we could visit tribes further within the island, but all that had changed. I had a couple of weeks to go before the flight home and was in no rush. Dave wanted to get back due to his business, but Sibu asked if he could join me for a spot of travelling. I was delighted. Over the next few days we flew to Sulawesi and visited the wonderful Torajan people, before nipping over to Java to visit the ancient Buddhist temple of Borobudur. Eventually we parted in Jakarta, where we had met just a few weeks before, but I had a funny feeling that we would meet again.

CHAPTER 8
MAROMOKOTRO
MADAGASCAR
OCTOBER 2007

"We never remember days, only moments"

CESARE PAVESE

Before I even start, let's get one thing clear. The island may be called Madagascar, but the people are not Madagascan. They are Malagasy. They don't have dancing lemurs or penguins and vanilla doesn't originate from there! Right, rant over...

It was with serious trepidation that I boarded the plane from Birmingham to Madagascar (via Paris). The final chapter in my Seven Mountains, Seven Islands challenge was about to begin and I felt unprepared. I had forgotten my best zoom lens, rushed to get to the airport and wasn't really sure what I had got myself into. Information about Maromokotro was sketchy and Jaime Vinals in Guatemala had been my best guide. He had been in Madagascar a couple of years before and gave me the best contacts to find. As ever he was right and I owe him a great deal.

The plane touched down safely in Antananarivo (commonly known as Tana) and I grabbed my bags before wandering out into arrivals. A scrum of people were waving banners, shouting loudly and offering taxis. This is not unusual in many parts of the world. I had already booked transport, but struggled through the intense heat and dust to make anything out. There I stood, sweating more and more, holding onto my kit for grim death and staring into the mêlée hoping for a saviour. One by one the people went until only two of us remained. Before me stood a silent Malagasy man holding a tattered taxi sign for a Mr Miguel Vardez...

I spent a night alone in a small hotel room. It was late, I was tired and already missing Tina. I had left her again and felt as guilty as ever. At least we could send the occasional text, but it was hardly a substitute for her laughter, heart and soul. I drank a cool beer before a fitful night's sleep.

I was awoken early by a knock at the door. "Mr Vardy, your taxi is here!" Time had flown by and I was late. I jumped out of bed, threw on my clothes, grabbed my bags and dragged them bouncing down the two flights of stairs to the waiting 2CV. The sun was blazing in the open concrete courtyard, but the air felt cool and refreshing. I was at over 1200 m (4000 ft) and the breeze felt wonderful. I hadn't realised how stuffy it had been inside my room. I was driven (if that's the word) back to the airport in a battered, yellow 2CV, which broke down almost instantly. Fortunately, it wasn't a major mechanical problem, just a lack of fuel. The driver was singing away quite happily to himself when the engine spluttered to a halt and casually opened the glove box to reveal a plastic drinks bottle full of petrol. He jauntily got out, refuelled and started up again. Just another day in the office for him. I don't think in all my years of travel that I have ever seen such a thing!

The flight north to Diego Suarez allowed terrific views of Madagascar's east coast. Vanilla plantations, remote reefs and sweeping coves seemed the order of the day. Palm trees waved in the sea breeze and holidaymakers relaxed on the pure sands. It all seemed idyllic and perhaps it was for beach goers, but I was here to climb, not laze about. Adrenalin began to flow through my body and pump my muscles for the final challenge. At home the media was unexcited, but out here in the Indian Ocean I was loving every moment!

After so many e-mails across the world, I was glad to finally meet Aristide Hery. He was to be my guide for the next couple of weeks and had helped Jaime when he had been here two years before. He was a Malagasy through and through, strongly built and stocky. He looked kind, relaxed and had a beaming smile, revealing brilliant white teeth. He spoke quietly and within seconds I knew we were going to get on handsomely. We had spent an evening in a small restaurant organising the last details of the trip when an unknown fact came to haunt me.

I knew the trip was two weeks. I knew the temperatures were going to be boiling. I knew the terrain would be difficult. What I didn't know was that we had to cover around twenty miles a day, every day, to complete the trip. Years ago that would have been simple, but my feet weren't what they were and boiling heat means my skin grafts suffer badly. The wounds swell and macerate easily, making them sore and weak. I sat and pondered the thought of tearing my heels apart over the next few days. I knew my injuries well, but had never expected this. There was little I could do but go for it. Worrying wouldn't get me anywhere and if I put my mind to it, I might just get away with it. The problem was the lack of medical aid if it all went wrong. In a westernised country we can call in the doctors, hop onto motorised transport or call an ambulance, but where we were going there was no road, no help and if my feet failed, no chance.

The next morning a couple of pick-up trucks appeared outside my hotel. Aristide had arrived with porters and gear ready, but needed some fresh food on the way. Everyone seemed happy enough, although none spoke any English. Still, I've always found that plenty of shoulder shrugging, smiling, pointing and eye rolling usually gets the message across. Whether it's the right message is another matter...

We left Diego at high speed on a well-surfaced and almost empty road, but one of Madagascar's major problems soon reared its ugly head. The tarmac began to peter away, leaving potholes and rocks in the highway. The tropical weather washes great swathes of the roads away every year, and keeping them open is a major job. It's a bit like the Alps in reverse, I suppose, just water doing the damage instead of snow and ice. Much of the rural traffic is drawn by animals or large tractors, which can cope well with the conditions, but we bounced around like pinballs for the rest of the day.

We stopped in a bustling market town for two of the most important provisions for the trip – live white chickens (more about them later) and sundried fish. Both were portable and a source of protein (at least that was my impression at the time). The market was full of colour, voices, aroma and flies. People waved and wafted over stalls of fresh meat and fish as the insect world did its best to settle down and lay eggs. The smell was overpowering, but part of life in the town. As travellers we have to accept the world for what it is wherever we are. I have never thought we have the right to tell others how to live their lives. Similarly, they have no right to tell us either.

We bounced around for another three hours, leaving the main highway and entering deep earth gullies just wide enough for our vehicles. They were dusty and solid, but I'm sure any rain would have turned them into channels of running mud and slurry. The soil was a deep red, which apparently is poor for agriculture, yet farm after farm began to appear. We crossed a muddy streambed, turned sharp left and entered what looked like a school compound in the village of Amborondolo. The engines went silent and our gear was thrown out onto the solid mud floor. I stood surveying my surroundings – a simple concrete school building, a few palms, jackfruits, a couple of sleeping dogs and the Mahavavy River. The ground was flat for miles around, but on the horizon I could see hills rising. "We can't see Maromokotro yet," said Aristide. "We will need to be much closer." Apart from ourselves, there wasn't a human in sight. The porters' chattering got louder and louder, as did their laughing. They seemed to tease each other relentlessly and I soon found out that two were cousins of Aristide's. I also noticed that they were all barefoot. Here I stood in my western leather boots, whereas they only wore what God had given them. I had turned out to be the one thing I had never wanted – a lone traveller with an entourage of porters in a foreign land. It might sound all very British explorer in the days of Empire, but actually I felt quite alone. I was missing Tina and for the next two weeks or so had no means of contacting her. Even a letter would have to wait to be posted upon my return and then it may take weeks to arrive.

I washed the dust off my sweaty skin with a swim in the river at sunset, before settling down to an excellent meal and then bed. There is no electricity for miles and therefore no lighting. The stars shone brilliantly, but by 8:30pm I was shattered and snoring.

Sleep is a vital part to any expedition. I was awoken early by a child's crying and couldn't rest again. I lay as long as I could before the boys stirred and the day began. It was barely dawn and the daily routine for the next few days was to become apparent. Up early for breakfast, strike camp and get moving asap. The dawn was cool, but by mid morning the sun would promise to be criminally hot. We had to be in camp before nightfall, with tents up and fires burning to eat before bed. That was how it had to be as the climate dictated the trip, not the people.

That first day's walk I was on the road before the sun rose. It was a beautiful and peaceful dawn, but as the sun began to rise the heat became oppressive. I have been to quite a few places in my time, but this was something else. I thought back to some of the islands I had travelled and compared the conditions – Baffin with its blizzards, Greenland with its glaciers, Japan with its rain and so on, but nothing was quite like this. I drank and drank, but couldn't keep up with my body's demands for water. I began to feel sick and by midday I had to get some cover. The lads were ahead of me and already had food and drink on the go in the shade of some trees. I was thankful of the cover as I was casting no shadow and melting on the spot. Oh, how I wished for a breeze, but there was not a breath. My feet were already aching and hot. I peeled off my socks and watched them dry before my eyes. My toeless feet caused a stir among the lads and they chatted away in Malagasy. I asked Aristide what they were saying. He replied that they were curious about what had happened to me, so with him translating, I tried to relate my frostbite on Mt McKinley story to them. Their eyes grew as large as eggs as Aristide described my ordeal. I don't think any of them could even imagine the cold I had been through, but their version of cold would be very much different to mine.

We set off after a couple of hours' rest and entered the crucible again. The dusty tracks were easy enough to follow as occasional tractors pulled trailers between the villages, laden with crops and farmhands. Everyone waved, some shouted, most were perplexed. What was a westerner doing here? I was asking that question to myself as the day wore on. The sun's power never seemed to wane and I was burning up. I sang to myself to keep in step and just kept going mentally. Two weeks of this promised to either make me or break me.

By early evening my legs were beginning to buckle. Aristide walked alongside me as the lads sped off to prepare for the evening. We talked about the environment and found a common interest. We were both passionate about nature and how we, as a species, treated it. Our backgrounds and cultures may have been vastly different, but our ideals were in the same place.

A few reed buildings appeared in front of us and I realised that we were almost done for the day. Within minutes we were in a small riverside village and only in the nick of time. Darkness was falling and my lonely head torch was the only electric light around. My body still reeked with sickness and I collapsed onto the floor and drank violently. I almost threw it all back out straight away, but held on, insisting to my stomach that I needed the refreshment. Only a few mouthfuls of food made it into my system, but as the coolness of the night came on, I began to feel a little better. A crowd started to gather to talk with the lads, but also to stare at me. I had become quite a novelty and the news of my arrival had spread like wildfire. There was a bit of a standoff due to the language barrier, but Aristide filled the gaps and once again I recounted my Mt McKinley story. There was much chatter and gasping as I tried to described what –60°C felt like in a country where frost was a legend.

I was sick in the night, but felt better for it. The air was stale and humid and again I had struggled to sleep. My alarm sounded at 5am and I woke in a foul mood. Diarrhoea had taken a hold of my system and I wasn't in the best of states for another thirteen days of this...

We ploughed on for four hours before the sun got too much to bear. Thankfully we stopped under a small grove against a peaceful river and I managed a little food, water and sleep. Aristide found a straw mat for me to sit on, which made all the difference. I rested my feet in the cooling waters, pulled on my socks and boots and set off for the afternoon. I looked at Aristide and asked, "How long this afternoon?" "Two and a half hours," he replied. I was soon to learn that this was Malagasy pace, not British. Memories of a jungle trip in the Amazon came to mind when the porters always told us that we were always "20 minutes" from camp, even at 10am!

The two and a half hours soon turned into four, even though I thought my pace good. Again, we were fighting darkness, but also the wind. A stiff breeze had blown up, making tent pitching difficult (and quite hilarious), but I did more than my share, helped cook and settled down after a relaxing river swim. I'm no great swimmer, but enjoyed the cool water as it ran over my dusty body, cleansed my wounds and brought goose pimples to my skin.

We had camped near two huge rock pinnacles, but last night's darkness had hidden them from view. The morning light revealed them in tremendous, dominating glory. They must have been a couple of thousand feet high, sheer, dark and eerie. [Insert Picture]

The river cut them clean in two, yet there was nothing else in its way for miles. Why hadn't it just gone around the bastion? A village stood on both sides of the wide and shallow river and legend has it that a family came here once to explore new farmland. A village was built against the shore, then one day the men went out to explore further. The river grew deeper; cutting them off from their homes and so another village grew on the opposite bank. Do I believe the story? Why not? I always like a good yarn and they are so important to many cultures across the world as a means of passing on tradition and knowledge.

Gently we began to climb into open grassland with the pinnacles still in view. They stayed with us until past midday and looked completely out of place. Aliens could have dropped them there for all I knew, but they were a tremendous way marker on our path. The country was changing and we were climbing into open highlands where the breeze was cooling and fresh. Long grass rippled like waves across the hillsides and rustled gently in the background. It felt so peaceful.

The day ended with a comedy river crossing on a bamboo raft. Well I say raft, more like half boat, half submarine. Even the porters looked worried as it wobbled across the river. One held kit, whilst one punted with a bamboo pole. I sat ready with my camera for the ensuing comedy fall, but it never happened.

Even I got across in one piece!

The next few days went on in a similar fashion. Early to rise, beating heat and starlit nights. We had to negotiate long granite slabs, cross more rivers and camp in sparser country as we gained height. I felt for the porters as their bare feet crossed awful terrain and I could see their shoulders were getting sore. There are no rucksacks here, just yokes flung over shoulders bearing terrible weight. I tried to carry one, but found it too much on my delicate western skin. They bore any pain silently, sang as they walked and laughed most of the evenings away.

Occasionally we met farmers, out on the trail looking for their zebu. They were simply dressed, usually in only a sarong, and carried huge amounts of rice, but little else. They had no shelters, emergency gear or means of communication, but they were together and knew their land well. They've probably been doing it for years. Some stayed for the evening with us (staring inquisitively at me), whilst others just waved and went on their way. To be honest, I was surprised to see anyone in this huge expanse of open land.

One party of three farmers sat with us in a small woodland clearing as evening fell. I noticed a young lad, perhaps in his early teens, who looked strong and able, but shy too. He sat with his eyes looking down as the others talked with the porters and I don't think he said a word. Occasionally he looked up, but would not make eye contact before darting his eyes down again. I felt for him, for as a child I suffered in silence, as my confidence was nil. For me, times have changed and I hoped they would for him. There's nothing worse than feeling the odd one out in a group. Of course, I could have been reading him wrong, but with no hope of conversing, there was little I could do but read his body language. As we cooked they looked longingly at our meal, simple as it was to us, but sumptuous to them. They only eat plain boiled rice, but we gave them some soup to at least flavour it. I don't think I could have eaten my chicken and vegetables next to them through sheer embarrassment if we hadn't at least made some gesture of goodwill.

During the journey in we had half a day off. My feet were happy for the rest, particularly as my left heel had begun to bleed a little. It was nothing serious as I had suffered it before, but in western climates, not tropical. Infection was always a risk, but I seemed to be ok, at least for now. I caught up with sleep, read a little and did something I have done for years – write my diary. I haven't missed a day since I was a teenager. Memories are important to me. My diaries sit stacked in my desk at home and one day may provide an insight into my life. Will I be lucky enough to have someone to pass them to?

And so the 12th of October came. Why am I marking out that date? It was summit day. We cut our way through thick bamboo groves listening to the lads singing happily away and entered a beautiful set of cascades. They were each only a few feet high, but were stepped a half-mile deep. The sound of falling water was music to my soul as we manhandled ourselves over fallen trees and stones to ascend them. The farmers' tracks had been left far behind as cattle seem not to venture this high. We waded upstream until the stream petered away and entered an unusually homely landscape. The bamboo and scrubland had been replaced by peat bog, cotton grass and granite outcrops. I stood and thought, "This is just like Kinder Scout or Bleaklow back in Derbyshire." Indeed it was, but 8000 feet higher. The squelch of peat crescendoed from my boots as it had done for countless years at home. I felt truly alive and smiled broadly. My challenge was about to end as if I were in the peaks of my childhood.

Maromokotro is a sacred mountain and some of the

porters wished not to climb it. I respected their decision and left them with the bags whilst Aristide, myself and a few others wandered uphill. It was more a stiff walk than a climb and we stepped over a summit ridge to see a tall, stone cairn standing in the distance. This was not the summit, but a marker made by a French climbing club. I approached it with a tingle of excitement in my heart, as the true summit was only yards away. I had a chance here to set a British climbing record, paid for and sorted mainly by myself. That in itself is a true challenge...

I stood on the summit at 12:08pm Madagascan time and claimed my prize, but something felt wrong and I couldn't place what it was. The summit had 10/1936 chipped into it – I assume the date when it was first surveyed? We were only at 2876 m (9436 ft), but I could have been on top of the world. Below me lay miles of empty grassland and jungle. I couldn't see a single sign of human habitation or disturbance. We were the only people for miles. A few pictures were taken and Aristide helped me shoot some video. I recorded a piece for Tina, as her thoughts had never left me for one moment. I would have loved her to have been with me, but that couldn't be. There are some things in life we have to do alone...

I unfurled my Union Flag for the final time on this challenge and thought about the long journey that had taken me here across the snows of the Arctic, the jungles of Asia and now the grasslands of Madagascar. It had been life changing, demanding and strenuous, but worth it.

Aristide donned a sarong and brought up a single white chicken (remember them?), some money and honey. He took off his shoes and blessed his ancestors, before pouring the honey on a rock and placing the money in a rusting enamel coated bowl. The chicken was released as per custom, but I wondered what it was going to do. It looked confused and huddled under a rock for shelter. A circling bird of prey had other ideas...

As with all mountains, the summit is only half the journey and we had a six- or seven-day journey back to civilisation to complete before the celebrations started. I quietly walked down the hill, back towards the porters and suddenly realised what was wrong with me. There were no tears of joy, no jumping around and screaming. My challenge was done and all I could think about was "what's next?" I needed a focus; perhaps another challenge in my life as this one had come to an end. I tried to pass it by, as there was still a great deal of walking to do, not realising what it was going to cost me later.

We camped just below the peak close to where a small stream flowed and settled down for the night. Even I wore a fleece jacket as the evening air began to bite, but I hardly realised what the temperature would do to my Madagascan companions. I drifted into a beautiful sleep, snug in my tent and sleeping bag, but woke to sounds of shuffling and whispering. I peered outside to see Aristide and the porters lighting a fire to keep warm. They were without thick clothing and shivered in a huddle as the flames began to rise. I smiled and slid back inside my tent, unable to do much for them.

We did not take the same path home as our outward journey. At first I thought, "What a wonderful idea. I'll see much more of the country this way", but the first day out almost changed my mind. A straight line of dense jungle stood before us and apparently there was a known path into it. The problem was finding it. Bamboo, vines and creepers don't mess about when it comes to recovering from man's exploits and we struggled for over an hour to find our way inside, our only guide being a few machete cuts on a tree.

In we went, expecting to be at a riverside by mid afternoon. I could see the very river valley we needed and it didn't seem too far away, but there was an awful lot of undergrowth between us. We moved quickly for a few yards, and then stopped due to dense bamboo groves. We hacked and bashed our way through, sometimes pushing each other physically onward. Again the ground would clear; again we would stop. The game of cat and mouse went on all day and the light began to fail. We had descended a few hundred feet along a wide ridge and could hear the river directly below us, but the darkness dropped like a stone and we were stuck. Aristide asked me to sit down and make myself comfortable whist he and a couple of porters cut their way through to the river. Out of the pitch black I occasionally heard shouts, but little else. There was hardly a star in the sky and once again, I had the only torch. I did see lights flicker from in between the trees, but I thought my eyes were deceiving me. They were not. The porters had made simple torches by tying bamboo shoots into tight bundles. They seemed to light well and provided at least a little guidance through the trees. There seemed more and more rustling and suddenly Aristide appeared before me. "Follow me, Nigel," he said. "We have found the river." Finding is one thing, but getting there is another. I turned on my head torch and followed Aristide down a steep muddy slope. You naturally dig your heels in when descending like this, but mine were sore and complained at every step. Still, we had to get to the river, firstly to camp, but also for drinking water.

The slope began to get steeper. I grabbed onto anything I could – trees, vines, bamboo – hoping to break any fall. I had no idea, in fact any care, if the branches were laden with thorns – I couldn't see a bloody thing. My head torch beam broke little of the darkness as leaves and branches flashed before my eyes. The air was filled with shouting, smashing foliage and running water. The river was getting closer, but the slide down was beyond a joke. Eventually I let go and slid on my backside the last hundred or so feet, stopping suddenly at the top of a small cliff edge. It was the riverbank. I swept the area with my torch and found the porters busily clearing an area for the tents. I was hot, sticky, dusty and covered in cuts, but thankful that the day was done. We had been in the jungle for over 15 hours.

The next morning it all seemed better. Bright sunlight, a good wash and hot food made all the difference. The problem was that we had no idea where on the river we were. Aristide was soon off and returned with good news. We were only about 500 yards off course and could follow the riverbed down. There was a village only a few miles further on and we could stop there for the night.

At times the river was chest deep and surprisingly cold for this part of the world. It felt refreshing though and certainly cleaned out yesterday's dust and grime. I paddled out of the far bank against a well-worn path covered in animal tracks – something we had not seen for days. We gathered ourselves and walked through deep grassland and pasture towards the village.

I heard a strange noise ahead. It was like something I had forgotten long ago – it was a woman's voice. For so long we had been only ourselves – a few men in the wilderness – but her voice broke boundaries in my mind. She appeared in moments, a young woman with three children. We smiled politely and Aristide said a few words as they passed by on their way to the river. The village was not far away...

We arrived mid morning and Aristide decided that we needed a day of rest. I certainly did as my feet were soaked and the skin grafts on my heels were suffering. Last night's epic had taken its toll. The digging in of boots had scraped them raw. The sun was warm, the people happy and the village busy. Again I seemed the centre of attention, as the last foreigner they had seen was Jaime, two years before. I opened up my video camera and turned the screen so that people could see themselves as I filmed them. A group of girls got very excited about it all, particularly when I played the film back. Perhaps a little purity in the world still does exist.

The day seemed to pass uneventfully, but in the evening I felt strange. For the first time in days I was sleeping under a solid roof. We were all laid out in a mud hut, which felt somewhat crowded, though in reality it wasn't. I had become so used to my own space in the tent that a solid structure felt invasive and my personal space invaded.

I lay in the dark for hours listening to the rustlings and snoring of the porters. What time I finally slept I'm not sure, but my mind milled around with the fact that my challenge was done and the trip was over, even though we still had a few days walking to do.

I expected a hot journey home, but the weather broke on the first day and brought torrential rain. Though I was prepared, the porters suffered as the cold soon crept through their poor clothing. We were still high in the mountains and a piercing chill soon entered the air. I drew clouds from my breath and felt my fingertips going numb. I just kept my head down and walked. Occasional people passed us by at great speed. The Malagasy people are fleet of foot, particularly in bad weather! I thought we had seen the last of them until we rounded a corner against a stream and were met by a huge overhanging boulder. Beneath the overhang were half a dozen folk all sheltering from the weather. A small fire was struggling to burn and throwing grey smoke out in long trails. We decided to camp against the boulder to at least give the porters a break from the incessant rain. I was soon sorted out and gave the lads a hand with their tents before we ate. The tents didn't look very waterproof and as I found out next morning, leaked like sieves!

I saw something incredible the next morning – a bicycle! I had heard a bell in the distance, but thought I was dreaming. Sure enough a classic sit-up-and-beg with a barefooted and smiling man on it came breezing by. He waved and was gone in a moment. So, civilisation was almost at hand. I drank beer that evening, saw electric light and realised that the modern world has a great deal to answer for. Are we improving or invading people's lives with our modern gadgets and methods? One for the philosophers I think. I slept in a bike shed and woke to the sounds of a tractor and trailer as they bounced past the shed on their way to the fields.

The next day I crossed the final river and entered a small town. The children cried "Vassa! Vassa!", which I assume means stranger or foreigner, but it was screamed with smiles and waves. A large market was bustling with local produce and the roads were packed with tractors and taxi buses. I sat down under a tree and gave away my walking boots to one of the lads. My feet were shattered, but there was no more hard work for them to do. I wished most of the porters goodbye and joined Aristide for the bumpy journey back to Diego. The language barrier may have prevented us from speaking, but a close bond had appeared between the porters and myself. I soon missed their kindness, laughter and infectious happiness.

Aristide drove me to the airport where my name changed again (I was now Nibble Vardy), before we wished each other goodbye. He had been a good guide and friend on my journey. We should respect the people who help us achieve our goals in life, rather than, as many do, pass them by.

And so my trip was done. I flew across to South Africa to meet up with Sibusiso Vilane and spent a few days with him and his family in Swaziland, before heading home a changed man. Everyone said that I was different, but I couldn't see what had changed. I soon found out from Tina. I seemed empty and drifting. The challenge had given me a purpose and that was now gone. The man on a mission was now a lost figure, grasping out for something to hold onto. Over the next few months, this was to be one of the major causes of our relationship ending.

What price can we put on adventure?

CHAPTER 9
NOW IT'S ALL OVER, WHAT DID I LEARN?

"Man is least himself when he talks in his own person. Give him a mask and he will tell you the truth"

OSCAR WILDE

I'm not sure about that Mr Wilde, as it's always hard putting your perspective down on paper for fear of offending someone, but by not doing it are we offending ourselves?

Reality is something I see people shying away from on a daily basis when it comes to family, life, money or work. We live in a real world where real things happen. All the advertising in the world will not make it better or worse, easier or harder. Agony on the glaciers of Greenland, swimming through the rivers of Borneo, falling through the jungles of Madagascar, all are real, inflict pain or injury and have to be faced. I'm going to be as real as possible over the next few pages and give my perspective on how the challenge affected my life and the lessons I learned from it...

When I returned home to the UK, I expected little media interest and that's exactly what I got. The local press were excellent as ever and I thank them for the support they have always given me, but setting a British record did little for my standing in mainstream society. Perhaps if I had returned half dead, been on a TV reality show or slept with a celebrity I would have done better. Luckily I had done the challenge for my own experience, learning and benefit rather than anyone else's. I think it's important that we do things in life for our own good and not to always please other people. That doesn't mean being selfish, as every day we do things to help others, but only we can experience first hand what a wonderful experience and journey life is. Back at home I quietly continued with my life and reviewed my last five years of world travel.

I have been lucky enough to always come home to a loving family. Quite how I would have managed without them I will never know. Through all my years of adventure they have been stalwarts of my cause, even if I have caused them a few tears when I have left for far away lands. My returns home have been met with open arms, beaming smiles and lots of tea! My continued travels still hinge on my family support.

I teach in schools across the UK and see too many youngsters with little in the way of help, either because of broken homes, poor aspirations or lack of interest. I do what I can to enthuse them about the world and how they can have a positive impact on it by their examples and actions, but as a society this is something we need to improve on. Trying to enthuse teenagers who are soon to be the third generation unemployed in their families isn't the easiest of tasks. I'm not here to point fingers of blame towards anyone, but ask that as a nation we pick up the gauntlet and inspire our children to do something positive with their lives.

Assumptions can change the way someone is viewed, even if they have no chance to defend themselves. Let me tell you how this affected me. I completed my challenge with little support from the outdoor industry and no sponsorship. I received help from a local company in the way of clothing and tents, but nothing from anyone in the way of funding. I paid for every trip out of my own pocket, which put severe financial constraints on my life for five years, but it was my choice. Knowing where the money comes from is vital in my view of the expedition world. I paid for it, so I had only myself to answer to if things went wrong. If someone else pays your way, it is possible to take your eye off the ball too easily. You also have to answer to others when disasters happen. Many people, however, assumed that I was heavily sponsored or rich, or both. I was publicly questioned on many occasions about why I was charging for lectures as people assumed someone else had picked up the bill. At the time I felt quite insulted to be even asked, although I have now cooled off a little. I'm not monetarily rich and have earned every penny I have ever owned in my life by hard work. This is another lesson I take into education as some people think the world owes them a living. It owes them nothing unless they are prepared to put their own effort in first. I would have never completed the Seven Islands challenge unless I had worked long and hard and put the hours in. I had to take responsibility for my actions, turn my ideas into reality and get off my backside to do it.

Of course, monetary cost is one thing, but there are the physical and mental costs too. Physically the challenge did me the world of good, well except for an appendicitis and a few mouthfuls of best quality Bornean river water, oh and borderline sunstroke, but otherwise I was in wonderful health. My wounds suffered, but were well managed and pampered by both excellent podiatrist care and myself. I can find no substitute for good old-fashioned physical exercise in improving the human body. I'm not a great lover of gyms, much preferring climbing, mountain walking and cycling. A healthy diet helps of course, but energy still needs to be burned.

Mentally I suffered afterwards, which was my entire fault as I lost focus, but I found a drive and direction during the challenge like I have never experienced in my life. Do we need a mission, a purpose, a goal in our lives? I believe as human beings we do, otherwise we will become stale and lost. It doesn't have to be a cross-world adventure, but perhaps the starting of a business, the raising of a family or the helping of others. The important thing is that we find what is right for us, not what someone else says. We must find the path that we need to follow and take a stand when it comes to breaking away from everyone else's direction. We are all wonderfully different and that makes the world such a beautiful place to be. Imagine if we were all the same; well I don't even want to think about it!

Ok, here comes a hard one – relationships. This challenge

was the catalyst for two failing. I'm not going to say that it was the be all and end all, but I have to be honest here and honesty is something I pride myself on. International adventure, accidents, remote locations, high mountains and little communication all played their part. I have met people who come out with statements such as "I took a choice between becoming a mountain guide or losing my wife..." "He could be a great ice climber, if only he would leave his family..." Life is down to choices and we need to make them in the cold light of day. What is really, and I mean really, important to us? A few weeks' adventure, a relationship, a family? Don't worry, I'm being no killjoy here, but we need to take responsibility for what we do and how we do it. There will be outcomes from our actions – are we prepared for them? Are we being unfair? I love travel and also would like a family. Do the two mix? I think that they can, provided we can all learn the 'U' word – understanding. No one can have everything his or her own way without someone else worrying, somewhere, but if we understand each other, life is good.

Believe me I have learned this one the hard way. I'm no hero, no martyr; just honest in the words I have written. I have experienced love, worry, fear and insomnia and also inflicted them on others by my actions. I have also climbed with hundreds of people with strong relationships and loving families who understand each other's values, passions and desires.

I have always been proud of my Derbyshire roots. My family have lived there for over 300 years, as I do now. The subject of where you come from always rears it head when I travel. Trying to describe where Derbyshire is to many people is hinged on the fact that it's down and right a bit from Manchester United, but I have met people who are almost embarrassed to admit their roots, or even come out with the phrase "Well, you will never have heard of it". Does that matter? Let me give you an example...

I was sitting in a hostel in the Japanese city of Kyoto with my friend Diane. We had just returned from Mt Fuji and were doing a bit of sightseeing. One evening a group invited us to join them for a drink. The usual conversations started and I asked the girl sat next to me where she had travelled from.

"You'll have never heard of it," she said.

"Ok, try me."

"It's tiny."

"Go on..."

"It's called Farnah Green."

"Is it near Hazelwood by any chance?"

Her jaw dropped. I continued...

"Does it have a pub called the Bluebell?"

"How do you know that?"

"Because I'm only down the road in Belper. I used to go to a café in Farnah Green as a child, but it's been gone for years. A new house has been built on it."

"I live in that house!"

The conversation continued for a good half an hour, as she was amazed that someone understood where she came from. Of course the chances of a meeting like that are rare, but nevertheless, we should never be embarrassed of our roots.

One or two people have asked me why I take a Union Flag up mountains when I climb. That's simple enough to answer – I'm proud of my country. I am disturbed by the way some people portray flag flyers as nationalists and particularly concerned as to why the Cross of St George has almost become a football battle pendant. I see thousands of national flags proudly flown across the world with little or no insult to others, so what is the problem in the UK? Why should we not fly our national flags with pride, recognising our people and our country?

As I mentioned earlier, I work with many schoolchildren and one of the most common questions I'm asked when introduced as a climber is, "Have you climbed Everest?" Let me answer that in the next chapter...

CHAPTER 10
WHAT'S ALL THIS EVEREST THING?

"It has become a veritable Circus Maximus"

GREG CHILD

The honest answer is "No, I haven't". The differing views and opinions I get from this reply have stunned me over the years.

I work a great deal in education and almost every time I speak in a school I get asked the question. As soon as the word 'No' leaves my mouth, many schoolchildren switch off or say "You can't be a climber then!" Why do they make this assumption? Is it their education? Media hype? Are they only impressed by the biggest/tallest/fastest in the world?

Some adults have a similar view, but say little as they are trying to be polite. However, I have still been dismissed many times. The thing that bothers me is that many of the critics are armchair hero's who have read a few books and seen some pretty TV documentaries, but not felt the cold and exposure of a mountainside.

I think the media have a lot to answer for here. They put people on pedestals for being on a TV talent show, singing a song or climbing one mountain. They easily forget the casualties, environmental damage and amounts of money thrown about in the pursuit of a single peak. Unfortunately, media interest brings with it the pursuit of fame. Modern society seems hell bent on Saturday night television and so called "celebrity' status. This has crossed into every genre of society; most of all adventure where certain mountaineers' have become fixated with their own image, celebrity and self-publicism.

More and more people throw themselves at the peak, but what training do many of them have? By the end of the 2008 climbing season, there had been 4,102 ascents to the summit of Everest by about 2,700 individuals with the peak claiming over 200 lives. I am of the view that in any theatre of the world, a solid apprenticeship in your subject is a must.

I was recently out with some friends having a meal in a pub. A tabloid newspaper was laid out on an adjacent table, open at a page which sported a frightening headline. It announced that a young lady had summited Everest after taking up climbing only a year before. She was portrayed as a heroine and the story was written in a typical overstated tabloid style. What you read into this depends on your point of view. As a climber I am very worried by such stories as it belittles much of the hard climbing and guiding carried out every day in the mountains. It also makes many unprepared people fill their minds with thoughts of climbing above 8000m. The training, funding and mental attitude needed for serious peaks is huge. Of course, I'm looking at this as a mountaineer. On the other hand, if you are climbing for your own personal reasons, then good luck to you. Many thousands of pounds for charity are raised every year through climbing, but must you take on such a challenge? There are plenty of other things to do out there. Perhaps you think me a mountaineering snob, well that's your choice, but I view life as services earned in the old-fashioned time honoured tradition.

Before anyone points the finger, I have used the press and media on many occasions. We have worked well together and created good working relationships, but I have never sensationalised my stories or used agencies to press home the point. I've had stories turned down many times and that's ok by me. I have no desire to make the front pages. I'm happier writing articles and letters. If they get published, well that's great...

There are of course many people who are badge collectors. They must have done this or that before they die, otherwise they have not lived a fulfilled life (or so they say), but what is fulfilment? Should we let others decide what our outcomes and lives entail, or should we have a choice? I have been lucky enough to travel across the world on a number of occasions and seen people living perfectly fulfilled lives in some of the most remote and deprived corners of our planet. Is it the fact that they view their priorities differently? I think it is. Here's a personal example. My Grandparents generation were local farmers, railways workers, miners and policemen. Work was vitally important, otherwise you didn't eat. Holidays were visits to family members at best. Were they unhappy? Of course not, because their aspirations were simple. My parents' generation pushed a little further as personal transport became cheaper and more available, but even then, it was visits to the seaside or places of interest. Only a few braved foreign travel. Now take a look at my generation. Airports are crammed, motorways jammed and life is a rush. More people seem to be suffering stress and living life at breakneck speeds armed with computers and mobile phones. When I walk through the mountains I see more and more people admiring eachothers solar panels, laptops and telephones, more than the mountains around them. I have climbed with people who have lost the plot because their mp3 player is flat or wont work at altitude! I have to ask myself the question "what are they are doing here?" Is adventure just an excuse to hang pictures on a wall when you get home? I feel there's more to life than that. To share experiences, reflect on your life and find some peace, are but a few of the things that I look for.

It is obvious that society has changed. People seem to want more and demand more and mountaineering is no different from the generation examples I have given you. When Mt. Everest was first climbed in 1953, the news set the world on fire, particularly as the news was announced on Queen Elizabeth II Coronation Day. People were in awe of such an achievement, but the credit goes to a hard working, well organised and experienced team who made a superhuman effort to stand just two people on the world's tallest piece of ground. Now we just need to make a phone call, pay a lot of money, do a minimum of training and off we go! Is it right? Would we expect Formula 1 Drivers, Tennis Aces or Downhill Skiers to do the same?

I'd like to bring in here a thesis written by Roanne Finch, entitled – 'Is it about being the first or about being the best?' I first met Roanne in late 2007 when she was researching the piece for her Dissertation at the University of Derby. When I began writing this book in early 2010 I had no ideas of creating a chapter on Everest, but the more I wrote and due to the experiences I had, the chapter became naturally born. I contacted Roanne and she kindly allowed me to reference her thesis to help with my work.

Taking on such a mountain is one thing, but are you prepared for the barrage of questions that will come your way? *"The most regularly and repeatedly asked question throughout mountaineering history has been the question Why? Why climb? Every mountaineer will have been asked this at some point during [their] career".* I certainly have on many occasions. *"It was in the context of such persistent questioning from a New York reporter about his reasons why, that [George] Mallory made the [now famous] remark that he was returning to Everest, "Because it's there".* Over 80 years later that remark still rings out at many interviews and conferences.

"Society's constant questioning is in part borne out of a dissatisfaction with the lack of concrete answers given". The modern world wants straight answers and solid facts (and they want them now), but they are not always possible. I remember well, lying in a hospital bed only a few hours after suffering

severe frostbite demanding answers from the Doctors. They had none. I was stunned. In this modern world, surely we could tell what was going to happen? When it was going to happen? I soon found that we couldn't. I learned a valuable lesson that day, which has stuck with me for the rest of my life.

When it comes to answering the great question of 'why', I feel many mountaineers are unable to explain themselves publicly, because they cannot explain their feelings, motives and passions. This is in no way a criticism as I have difficulty explaining this myself, yet inside there is a force that drives me. *"For society, there will never be a satisfactory response to the question why and mountaineers' motivations will always remain incomprehensible as their actions completely contradict accepted social conventions and norms".*

"It defies the collective consciousness of man's primitive innate desires and inborn needs that individuals would willingly deny themselves, or at the very least severely curtail, their basic physiological needs (warmth, food and shelter)", and openly reject safety and security by not only putting themselves in precarious, life-threatening situations, but seemingly actively seeking this danger and risk out". Or should I put this point another way? Should the people who choose the more extreme environments of the world be well prepared, experienced and able to do so? Perhaps I sound elitist, but I would never ask anyone to do anything they weren't happy with. At times we go into uncomfortable and difficult situations, but we do that to challenge ourselves, both mentally and physically. Here again, I go back to serving that vital apprenticeship in the hills.

Does society struggle with the fact that we are not the norm they expect everyone else to be? Is it a problem that many people in this world want to seek out an escape from society to feel again the world's organic side? I just wonder if the Everest bug is caught up in this. Are people trying to prove how hard they are (or think they are) by attempting to climb her?

I recently talked with South African climber Cathy O'Dowd. Being the first woman to climb Everest from both sides gives her a great understanding of the difficulties of the mountain, yet she openly says that the mountain isn't the greatest difficulty. It's the team around you and how they work together, but that is another subject...

Something I agree with and indeed have personally found is that mountaineers are *"treated with awe and reverence, admired for their heroic feats and great acts of derring-do, and at the same time derided, mistrusted, viewed with scepticism and scorn. Fundamentally they have been seen as the other, both cast aside by and set apart from society as Outsider figures for the simple fact that they choose to rebuff accepted social conventions and norms and to flout the rules and regulations. True, many mountaineers have taken on the iconic status of being somewhat wild and rebellious, but it is typically borne out of a reaction against the constraining and increasingly restrictive impositions that are enforced by the organising authorities and institutionalised governance of society"*, but I feel much of this is a reaction to society's ever (and over) restricting views.

"Hillary had unexpected fame and celebrity thrust upon him with great pomp and ceremony by an excited public and press; made all the more poignant a triumph coinciding as it did with the coronation of the young Queen Elizabeth II: "a new, timely and brilliant jewel in the Queen's diadem" read the opening line of the Guardian leader when the news broke (in Nelsson 2007:110)". A great headline indeed, but it was hard for the other half of the summit team to comprehend what was about to happen as he descended the peak. Tensing Norgay

summited as a climber, but returned home revered as a God and found both Nepal and India fighting for his citizenship. He struggled with the fame instilled on him and I highly recommend reading the book "Man of Everest" by James Ramsey Ullman as an enlightening look into Norgay's life. Again we are back in the media. Does the modern Everest climber look back at the first ascent and hope for further fame? In my view, if they do, they are deluding themselves.

In the past, many Climbers or Mountaineers would have learned their trade on local rocks or hills and then hired guides to push themselves further. This is something I have done many times myself. I learned from guides the more technical skills of ropework in summer and winter conditions, fitting belays, digging snowholes and coping with the larger challenges the outdoor world can bring. "*Whereas many amateur mountaineers would previously have paid to be guided up Mont Blanc, the Matterhorn and other notable peaks as required by the progression demanded of what Kane & Zink (2004) termed "a serious leisure career" before attempting Everest, now Everest is the be all and end all, and no experience is needed*". A trek up Aconcagua (6962m) in Argentina has traditionally been the only requirement required and this is purely to test you at altitude.

I have undertaken many guided trips over the years, due to the remoteness of the areas in which I have travelled and for the safety and skills element, but there have been disturbing stories of people not knowing how to climb. When I say that, I talk of folk who don't know "*how to put their crampons on (one individual reportedly put them on upside down)*", or use ropes and knots correctly. I met a chap on the Hornli ridge of the Matterhorn who had no idea how to put a harness on, but was happy to be guided to the summit! "*The inability* and ineptitude of the prospective Everest summit bidder is an increasing cause for concern. Now, with no experience necessary, the paying clients are nothing more than tourists who have paid for an adventure experience".

"Ask any of the number of mountaineering adventure tourists whose gaze is firmly fixed on climbing Mount Everest why they choose to climb the mountain and the answer will invariably be the same: 'because it's the biggest.' As the highest point on earth Everest is the ultimate symbol of status and power."

The general public still believe that "Everest remains to be seen as the high point, the crowning glory, of any true, great mountaineer's career, [however] for many in the mountaineering community Everest has never held that great an appeal; because it is not that challenging. It is here that the void between the public's perception of mountaineering and the mountaineer's own understanding and appreciation of his craft is at its greatest. As the biggest, Everest is seen by society to be the best, the hardest, the most difficult and challenging test for a mountaineer". In fact the Debretts Guide for the Modern Gentleman lists climbing Everest as one of its Ultimate Challenges!

"Contrary to popular belief, height does not denote difficulty. The 'lesser' peaks of K2, Annapurna and Nanga Parbat pose far greater challenges than Everest; specific routes up mountains and their infamous north faces prove far more technically difficult than Everest's classic route of the South Col".

In 2009 I attempted to climb the SW ridge of Ama Dablam using the dodgy and worn fixed ropes (so dodgy and worn that one snapped and I took a fall above camp 2). The guides openly said that she was a much more challenging and interesting climb than Everest (one of the guides had summited Everest 6 times). Though fixed ropes exist on many mountains in some shape or form, people with little mountaineering experience or background rarely tackle them (the only exception I can think to this are the Via Ferrata routes of the Alps and the Dolomites). Many fail to summit Everest due to jams of people waiting to climb or descend the fixed ropes. The weather is critical to any mountain ascent, particularly at altitude, as is the thinness of the oxygen content in the air. Bottled oxygen has moved on in leaps and bounds from the early days of steel and aluminium cylinders, to modern composite and light materials allowing the Death Zone to be tackled by the masses. Unfortunately, many have run out of Oxygen due to delays on the fixed ropes and suffered the consequences. The Death Zone is usually agreed to be at 8000m and many deaths have been caused because the human body cannot acclimitise at such altitude. The body uses up its store of oxygen faster than it can be replenished, hence an extended stay in the zone without supplementary oxygen will result in deterioration of bodily functions, loss of consciousness and ultimately, death.

"While Everest retains its enigmatic status among the masses, for the mountaineer it has all but lost its magnetic qualities for there remain scant few unknowns: the mountain's major puzzles have long been unlocked. In all there have been fifteen routes forged to the top (Klesius 2003). Interestingly as Unsworth (2000:1, Appendix 5) observed, as the ascents via the classic route have risen dramatically of late, so, conversely." One recent trend has been a sharp decline in attempts and ascents of the more challenging routes – out of 327 ascents between 1997 and 1999 seasons only three climbers reached the summit by a way other than the standard routes from Tibet and Nepal." For the mountaineer, even the technical routes have lost their appeal. The most climbed mountain in

the world has quite simply been climbed to death".

Risk and mountaineering go together. We have to accept that as a fact, but we must never become complacent or we will feel their wrath (and the mountains can be very unforgiving). To many, mountaineers play with risk to feel the rush of adrenalin, even to become "Junkies". Society always wants to have its views here, but I would answer them by simply stating the fact that the most dangerous thing you will probably do in your life is drive a car. Careering at 70mph down a tarmac road in something weighing in at over a ton and talking on your mobile telephone (as I still see every day) puts mountaineering's risks into proportion. I'd like to see the critics give up driving and then I'll listen seriously to their views...

May 11th 1996 sums it up for me. 8 deaths in a single day due to bad weather, bottlenecks on the fixed ropes (34 attempting the same summit day), people summiting way past the allotted cut off time and reports of climbers not being experienced. Larger numbers exist on many of the world's peaks, but retreat is easier and they are not in the Death Zone.

I'm sure there have been much worse disasters during the annuls of mountaineering, but here the media jumped on the bandwagon and the disaster was broadcast around the world on TV and spawned many books and articles. To this day the disaster is still a contentious issue.

Personally I have no interest in climbing Everest and though I have wandered here, there and everywhere in this chapter, I believe the following statement sums up the Everest problem very simply...

It *"provide[s] "public interest", but distort[s] the "true values of mountaineering into an ego-driven media circus.""*

If that statement doesn't sum it all up, nothing will...

Printed in Great Britain
by Amazon.co.uk, Ltd.,
Marston Gate.